MW00846838

THE WORKBOOK
FOR SELF-MASTERY

By John Randolph Price

BOOKS
*The Abundance Book
Angel Energy
The Angels Within Us
*Empowerment
*The Love Book
*The Meditation Book
*Practical Spirituality
*A Spiritual Philosophy for the New World
*The Success Book
*The Superbeings
*The Wellness Book
*With Wings As Eagles
*The Workbook for Self-Mastery
(formerly The Planetary Commission)

SELECTED AUDIOCASSETTES
*The 40-Day Prosperity Plan
*A Journey into the Fourth Dimension
*The Manifestation Process
*Prayer, Principles & Power

Check your bookstore for the books and audios above.
Items with asterisks can be ordered through Hay House:
(800) 654-4126 • (800) 650-5115 (fax)

Please visit the Hay House Website at:
www.hayhouse.com

THE WORKBOOK
FOR SELF-MASTERY

A Course of Study on the Divine Reality

JOHN RANDOLPH PRICE

Hay House, Inc.
Carlsbad, CA

Copyright © 1997 by John Randolph Price

Published and distributed in the United States by:
Hay House, Inc., P.O. Box 5100, Carlsbad, CA 92018-5100
(800) 654-5126 • (800) 650-5115 (fax)

Edited by: Jill Kramer   *Designed by:* Jenny Richards

All rights reserved. No part of this book may be reproduced by any mechanical, photographic, or electronic process, or in the form of a phonographic recording, nor may it be stored in a retrieval system, transmitted, or otherwise be copied for public or private use—other than for "fair use" as brief quotations embodied in articles and reviews without prior written permission of the publisher.

The author of this book does not dispense medical advice or prescribe the use of any technique as a form of treatment for physical or medical problems without the advice of a physician, either directly or indirectly. The intent of the author is only to offer information of a general nature to help you in your quest for emotional well-being and good health. In the event you use any of the information in this book for yourself, which is your constitutional right, the author and the publisher assume no responsibility for your actions.

Library of Congress Cataloging-in-Publication Data

Price, John Randolph.
    The workbook for self-mastery : a course of study on the divine reality /
John Randolph Price.
        p.   cm.
    Rev. ed. of: The planetary commission.
    Includes bibliographical references.
    ISBN 1-56170-362-1
    1. New Thought.   I. Price, John Randolph. Planetary commission.
II. Title.
BF639.P855   1997
299'.93--dc21
                                                    97-12686
                                                    CIP

ISBN 1-56170-362-1

01 00 99 98   5 4 3 2
First Printing, June 1997
Second Printing, August 1998

Printed in the United States of America

*This book is lovingly dedicated
to the great Awakening that is under way,
moving us from illusion to Reality
and the rediscovery of
Who and What we are
in Truth.*

CONTENTS

◆ ◆ ◆

INTRODUCTION

◆ ◆ ◆

In our mortal slumber, we have crossed the borderland many times in search of ourselves, intuitively knowing that we are on a journey—someday to reach our destination and fully awaken to our true Identity.

In the invisible realm, we did not find a heaven or hell; our consciousness remained as it was on the material plane, with only the inconvenience of space and time removed. From the teachings of the Masters, we caught a glimpse of the Self we were created to be, and we knew that we were in the process of unfolding, reaching out toward the ultimate moment of Christhood—a term used hundreds of years before Jesus's time to mean the realization of the inner Self or True Nature of individual being.

Knowing that the interaction of our thought, feeling, and physical natures will accelerate our awakening, we chose to incarnate again on the physical plane. And here we are today, looking for the answer, seeking the solution, searching for the magic balm that will transform sickness to health, lack to abundance, discord to harmony. We have prayed, meditated, denied, and affirmed. We have imaged our good, spoken the Word, and pressed onward. Some of us have risen above the illusion and have seen the Reality. For others, the door to the inner Kingdom was jarred ever so slightly, and a shaft of Light penetrated into consciousness. The channel for expression was opened, only to be closed again by fear—yet when only a particle of Light was released, the needed money appeared, the healing took place, the relationship was harmonized, the job was found. But why be satisfied with only temporary relief? Why be content with a morsel when we can enjoy the feast that has been prepared for us since the beginning?

Since the knowledge of who and what we are is the key to the Storehouse, let's pause briefly for a review.

We were created by God and eternally remain as God in expression—as the radiant Master Self, Spirit, or Soul we are in truth. (I use *Self, Spirit, Soul,* and *Divine Consciousness* interchangeably.) There is no other Self. What we call our "personality" is an energy field of a higher and lower vibration. The higher is consciously aware of Spirit-Self and resonates with Truth, while the lower listens to the fear and falsity of what we know as ego, a thoughtform of misqualified energy that we created in the sleep state under the illusion that we were a physical body. The higher mind of individual consciousness as God-Light maintains our identity as individual *I* and listens to the knowing of Spirit as complete fulfillment. The lower self-created emotional mind of personality (ego) maintains the illusion of a physical being forever seeking the fulfillment of needs.

In our original state, we knew our Self to be the perfect creation of, and forever one with, Supreme Being. When we came to dwell in the material plane and took on a physical body, a part of our Divine Consciousness was lowered in vibration for the purpose of grounding and functioning on the third-dimensional plane, and for a time there was no sense of duality, no separation in consciousness. Our Self-awareness became the medium between Spirit and the material world, interpreting spiritual ideas as form and experience. We lived under grace—the love of God in action.

Eventually the vibration of Self-awareness—that higher mind of personality—became conscious of only the third-dimensional world. From the realm of grace, we descended into the province of karma and came under the law of cause and effect. Now there was a sense of separation as the Holy Self remained one with God, while our awareness of the truth of being dropped further into darkness. That is when we formed the ego and began to entertain concepts of materiality. Soon we identified only with our physical bodies and with our creations in the world and began to create selfishly. Competition was born. Then destruction, and protection from destruction. The world began to reflect this consciousness. Plants took on briars and needles, insects formed stingers, and poison came forth in reptiles. Self-preservation became the basic instinct of animals and human beings. Fighting began, and the illusion of death, which was never a part of the Divine Plan, became an apparent reality.

Fortunately, this scenario does not have to continue. For eons, the Masters have shown us that we can live on a higher frequency and enjoy a world—a *physical* world—where love, joy, and peace abide in a life truly more abundant, a life without the slings, arrows, and scarcities we have grown to know so well. And we find that world when we get the ego under control, move back into a conscious awareness of the Holy Self within, and become clear channels for the divine expression—which includes everything we could possibly desire in this lifetime. We can touch heaven right where we are as we move from the lower vibration of personality to the higher and remain there until that moment of supreme realization where there is only one I AM—I AM *THAT* I AM—and all sense of separation is dissolved. Then we can say with true spiritual integrity—with *understanding*—"I and the

Father are one; therefore, there is now only the Reality of Oneness." This is the moment of Christhood, and through this collective *Second Coming* in mind and heart, the entire world is lifted up into a new dimension of wholeness.

Step One in the Process Is an Understanding of the Cosmic Will-to-Good

It is suggested that you purchase a spiral-bound notebook to serve as your *Workbook for Self- Mastery*. Your workbook should be separated into four sections titled: (1) Lessons to learn and lessons learned, (2) My gifts and talents, (3) My life program, and (4) Knowing myself. Each section will represent a part of your Master Plan for this particular lifetime.

To plan something means to conceive, to think out, to make arrangements for—and the sum total of the conceiving, the thinking, and the arranging constitutes the plan. From a universal perspective, we can see that the *Divine Plan* is the strategy and blueprint for each individual man and woman, for the entire human race, and for the planet itself, as conceived by the Infinite Thinker. In essence, we are talking about the *Will of God*, and if we think of that Will as the cosmic urge to express infinite Good-for-All, we begin to sense the absolute magnificence of the Plan: Peace and harmony, breathtaking beauty, omnipresent unconditional love, overflowing abundance, radiant perfection in mind and body, a true place of total fulfillment for each individual, unlimited joy and perfect order, and the ability of each Divine Expression of this Infinite Mind to co-create with wisdom and understanding in revealing God's Kingdom on Earth.

How do we get back in tune with that Divine Plan, that Will-for-Good in our lives? By developing our own Master Plan, our own personal Workbook for Self-Mastery. Remember that we have lost our awareness, understanding, and knowledge of ourselves as perfect expressions of God; we are literally asleep to our True Nature. But as we seriously consider a new agenda for our lives and dedicate ourselves to the Truth, we will begin the awakening process—an awakening to our reason for being here now and the overall purpose of this incarnation. Thus, our Master Plan will be a teaching model with various learning experiences to help us clean up and clear out consciousness, leading us directly into an understanding of God's will for us as individuals.

In Part I of this book, we will cover three of the four sections that you will be concentrating on in your workbook, including the lessons, your gifts and talents, and the life program. In Part II, which is considerably longer and more detailed, we will concentrate on *feeling* the Truth, *knowing* the Truth, and *being* the Truth. That is why the most important signpost on the spiritual path reads "KNOW THYSELF." And the reason for this admonition: We cannot expand consciousness into the *universal* until we understand and realize the true nature of the *individual*.

As you pursue the spiritual activities in Part II, please remember to write in your workbook the thoughts, feelings, images, and ideas that come to mind. This will assist in the retraining and renewing of mind and emotions and lift you up into that higher frequency where you may participate in the healing of this world, the transforming of the collective consciousness, and the revealing of the true reality. And that is what Part III of this book is about—your role as a planetary healer.

Let's get started.

PART I

THE
DIVINE PLAN

*"Have a purpose in life, and,
having it, throw such strength of mind
and muscle into your work
as God has given you."*
— Thomas Carlisle

CHAPTER ONE

◆ ◆ ◆

LESSONS TO LEARN,
LESSONS LEARNED

In the implementation of the plan for your individual life, between incarnations you have the opportunity to choose those experiences and conditions that will help you in your spiritual growth. Each experience is a lesson, and each lesson learned will awaken certain spiritual qualities that are a part of your true nature. This is all contained in your individual Akashic Record, which shows your existence as a spiritual being, the slipping into the dream state, your miscreations and the karmic effect, the series of lessons undertaken to eliminate karma and awaken to Truth, and the record of your journey thus far. Prior to each incarnation, your Record is reviewed for you, and you choose the lessons for your next lifetime in physical form.

One of the most efficient ways in pinpointing lessons to be learned is to take a close look at your astrological sun sign. In the book *Esoteric Astrology*, we read: "This sign indicates *the present* problem of the man; it sets the pace or the established tempo of his personality life; it is related to quality, temperament and the life tendencies which are seeking expression during this particular incarnation..."[1] And Dr. Douglas Baker, English author and teacher of Ancient Wisdom, writes: "Birth in each Sign of the Zodiac provides certain qualities of environment and opportunity to develop the physical, emotional and mental vehicles. ...There is learning by 'trial and error'...to distinguish between what brings pleasure and what brings pain."[2] For the purpose of our analysis, I have listed particular lessons for each sun sign. Find yours and record the pertinent information in your workbook.

ARIES: The lesson to learn in this energy is to be self-confident and independent, with great initiative to find optimum harmony, balance, and true purpose in life. If this is not accomplished through spiritual disciplines, one may be vulnerable to excess, disorder, disruptive impulsiveness, insufficient willpower, and a lack of focus on a definite purpose. Those born under this sun sign came to learn self-restraint, self-control, and self-direction—with calmness and consideration for others.

TAURUS: The primary lessons to learn include mastery of the quality of spiritual will and power, and the development of a consciousness of the Spirit within as both the giver and the gift, the supplier and supply, thus becoming a master of financial matters. To do so, one must move beyond an overemphasis on materialism, self-indulgence, misjudgment, and the conflict between mind and emotions which results in such contradictory mood swings that family, friends, and associates are baffled by the insults one day and praise the next.

GEMINI: Those with this sun sign volunteered to partake of the Gemini energy in order to bring a harmonious synthesis into life. They seek to master the divine-earthly duality, and learn the wisdom of the ages and clear judgment in order to be an instrument of creative goodwill. In learning the lessons, they will overcome scattered thinking and lack of concentration, the inability to feel deeply and express true affection, and a sense of pessimism and cynicism.

CANCER: The objective in this sign is to learn tenacity, to heighten the feeling nature while maintaining control of reactive emotions, and develop the quality of nourishing love. On the negative side, one must understand that living in the past is a detriment to spiritual growth, and that selfish egotism, a desire for power over others, hypersensitiveness, and feelings of martyrdom must be overcome in order to find the true Light of Self.

LEO: The energy of this sun sign provides the individual the opportunity to embody the qualities of strength, power, and will—to move through life with great courage, composure, and poise. It is a free and joyous energy, and gives the individual a sense of dignified ease while expressing true love in action. One must be careful, however, because this same energy can also be used harmfully as arrogance, dishonesty, cruelty, and a self-centered attitude with peacock vanity.

VIRGO: Those born under this sign came to learn the mental-emotional disciplines required for good physical health. It is an energy of cleansing and purification and enables the individual to be less body conscious and more aware of the indwelling divinity. It is also the quality of discrimination, order and efficiency, and detail-mindedness. In mastering these lessons, one must be careful not to take on an attitude best described as cold, cynical, crafty, overly critical, and selfish.

LIBRA: The lesson here is balance and harmony in all aspects of life, which leads to peace, joy, and love as the forces of thinking, feeling, and willing are equalized. The energy of Libra is justice, compassion for others, peace without conflict, poised power, and true success in creative endeavors. In taking the Libra course, one can be vulnerable to aloofness, an overattachment to the body, a wasting of time and a scattering of forces, and a reliance on past success rather than taking new roads to creative fulfillment.

SCORPIO: Scorpio is the energy of death and rebirth, and those who chose this sign for incarnation did so to move beyond the lower desire nature, to self-control in the light of Spirit. It is the sign of the warrior seeking the death of the murderous, selfish, lustful desires of the lower appetites of past lives and a new birth into the truth, joy, power, and freedom of the spirit of the eagle. To pass the test, one must overcome jealousy, malice, envy, and revenge, and climb the mountain into the higher energies of this regenerative sign with patience and perseverance.

SAGITTARIUS: The course lesson for the Sagittarian is the illumination of the intellect with the goal of reaching spiritual consciousness. One learns the qualities of divine inspiration, joyous optimism, freedom and independence, and total confidence in fulfilling aspirations. It is the ideal of living on the physical plane while seeing the reality of the spiritual world in and through all form. In mastering this energy, there will be a vulnerability to materialism, excessive physical activity, explosive indignation, righteous anger, criticism, and malicious talk.

CAPRICORN: This is the energy of ambition turned inward toward the Divine Self, and the power of authority to move through obstacles and achieve spiritual realization. In the outer world, the energy will take one into positions of leadership and responsibility under the guiding light of spirituality. The lesson is to learn true selfless service to others through persistence and concentration. If the energy is misqualified through utterly selfish ambition and desires, the individual will be mired in the darkness of deception, egotism, fanaticism, and materialism.

AQUARIUS: Love is the lesson of Aquarius—unconditional love for all of humankind. Through this energy, the individual is able to bring ideals into reality for the universal good through the spirit of love and truth. The Aquarian course teaches joyfulness bordering on frivolity, altruism, genuine friendship, and the dignity and spiritual equality of all people regardless of race, color, creed, or nationality. The lower manifestations of this energy include inertia, antisocial behavior, a high degree of impatience, a fiery temper, and a tendency toward anarchy.

PISCES: Those who have elected to take this course did so to have a greater understanding of the purposes of life and to develop a proper perspective of the individual's relationship to the world at large. The energy stabilizes mental forces with practical thinking, builds faith, strengthens integrity, brings up deep feelings of forgiveness, and offers a sense of true destiny relating

specifically to the emerging Christ spirit. Its negative characteristics are emotional suffering, a victim consciousness, and the
belief that outside forces are the masters of life.

What are your lessons to learn in this particular incarnation?
Look at your sun sign, meditate on the question, and record your
answers in your workbook.

**You can also look at the karmic wheel of your life for the
answers.** Visualize a large Ferris wheel, with each compartment
filled with human experiences. As the giant wheel rotates, see the
lowest compartment, the one closest to the ground, tip over and
release certain conditions and experiences in your life, and then
move on. If you will analyze your life, you will find that as your
karmic wheel makes its rotation, it will usually discharge conditions and circumstances of a similar nature. For example, you
may have faced financial problems and found a way to overcome
them, only to be troubled with additional experiences of lack as
the wheel comes back around again. Or perhaps it's relationship
or health problems that seem to be cyclical in nature in your life.

Take time now for a review—going back as far as you can
remember. Make a list of the more traumatic experiences, those
of a highly charged negative nature. Note the approximate year
and the general circumstances involved in each one. Do not be
concerned about drawing negative energy into your consciousness by bringing each experience back into your mind. They are
all still there, all securely deposited in the appropriate container
on your wheel, so bring them out on paper in the first section of
your workbook, and take a close look at them.

A little memory jogging may help you. Think about this
question: "What has been the major manifest problem in my
life?" Consider:

- *Personal relationships*

- *Job and career fulfillment*

- *Health and physical well-being*

- *Financial abundance and security*

- *Safety and protection*

Add other conditions and circumstances that have been expressed in your life as negative experiences.

Now please answer this question: "What do I fear the most in my life?" Is it the fear of being lonely? A fear of failure? A fear of lack? A fear of disease? Name your fears and write them down in your workbook. The objective is to see if your fears tie in with the major manifest problems in your life. It may take a bit of analysis on your part, but it will be well worth the time and effort.

For the next part of lessons to be learned, answer this question: "What do I consider the major flaws of my human consciousness?" You may want to consider one or more of the following:

- *Selfishness*

- *Jealousy*

- *Resentment*

- *Dishonesty*

- *Inertia*

- *Spiritual pride*

- *The inability to express love*

- *An inability to receive*

- *An inability to give*

- *Feelings of unworthiness*

- *Possessiveness*

- *Cynicism*

- *Anger*

- *Other—(continue with your own personal evaluation of your consciousness)*

Now let's put it all together and answer this final question: "In looking at the energy opportunities of my sun sign and the manifest problems that keep recurring, in examining my major fears, and after taking inventory of the major flaws in my consciousness, what are the lessons I must learn in this incarnation in order to move fully into spiritual consciousness?"

Let me give you an example of what one particular answer might be: "I see that I came into this world to master the meaning of love, which obviously I have failed to do because my karmic load in this incarnation has been one of relationships and the ability to relate to others in a loving and meaningful way. This ties in perfectly with my great fear of being alone, particularly in my later years in life. And as a result, I am possessive in my relationships, frequently jealous for no apparent reason, and filled with self-doubt and a lack of self-worth when the relationship falls apart."

The lesson for this individual is *unconditional love*, loving Self and others with no strings attached. In this particular case, the lesson to be learned was obvious, but in many others it is not. So when it just doesn't stand out in light, you may have to go back and trace the root cause of the condition. For example, do the physical problems seem to always occur during or following a financial crisis? Did the string of broken relationships result in job dissatisfaction and unfulfillment in your career? Many people can track a problem back to one particular vulnerability, and in a great number of cases, it has been a problem related to financial lack. One friend of mine discovered in his life-scan that most of the crisis situations during his adult years could be traced to financial insufficiency. In almost every instance relating to career unfulfillment or physical ailments, the root cause was concern about money. So he knew what he had to learn in this lifetime: the laws of spiritual abundance.

Like the individual with the relationship problem, your list may reveal negative experiences all grouped under one heading. Perhaps it's health. If other problems seem to be only side effects of this major challenge, then you know that you chose to realize God as your life and the perfection of your body in this incarnation. Or, there may be a record of continual dissatisfaction with the jobs you've had and with your career in general. This discontent could be a signal that your purpose in this lifetime is to find your true place—that circle of light where your divine plan can be expressed most effectively. Whatever the common pattern of less-than-desirable circumstances may be, now is the time to do something about it. If you wait, you will simply have to go through the same thing all over again.

Another point to consider: Every negative experience or pattern on your karmic wheel is directly related to your concept of your own self-worth. What you really believe about your own worthiness is externalized in your life and affairs. If you feel unworthy in any area of your life, you have added a burden in the form of a karmic debt, and it must, by law, be outpictured in your affairs.

When you begin to equate your worthiness with God's worthiness, realizing that you are an Individualization of the Creator of this universe, the debts are paid and you are free. When you know yourself, you will have mastered your lessons, so think about the idea that you are living right now. Do you see yourself as the spirit of God, God in individual expression? If not, do not waste another moment living the idea that you are just a "human being." Take the idea that God is individualized as you, and let your thoughts flow from that state of consciousness. Let your emotional nature *feel* according to that Truth. Let your words reflect the totally unlimited Being that you are, and let your actions be based on the Truth that you are Omnipotence made manifest! When you live the idea that you are the Christ of God, the law will create everything in your life to reflect that idea—abundance, love, bodily perfection, true place, success, great joy, total peace, enthusiasm, beauty, and the kind of livingness that was planned for you in the beginning.

Cutting the cord. What about karmic links of a negative nature to another person? These were obviously created in the past through resentment, hostility, and fear, and you may have drawn these people back into your life so that you could learn the lesson of forgiveness. If you work daily and diligently with cleansing meditations, forgiving the past, and asking your

Master Self to eliminate all error patterns and negative emotions, the remnants of those karmic links will be dissolved. But if you continue to plant seeds of condemnation and unforgiveness, you will be canceling out the releasing action and maintaining the status quo.

One way to cooperate with Spirit is to cut the psychic links that bind you to the other person. Just imagine that there is an energy cord (and there definitely is) between you and the particular individual. You are literally "linked up"—tied together—by a cord of negative energy attached to the solar plexus of both parties. You must *want* to cut that cord, and you must take the action to do it. Take an imaginary pair of scissors in your hand and cut the cord now. See it snap—feel it break. Your consciousness will instantly respond to this mental-emotional action, but you must see the cord break in your mind's eye. Once it is severed, begin to pour out all the unconditional love you can feel and send it to the other person. He/she has been released from you and has been moved out of your energy field to experience only the highest good. The attachment has been severed for the good of all concerned, and both of you are free. Now you can love unconditionally with no strings attached.

You are not here to suffer. The Divine Plan for you does not have a special section on suffering. While the law of cause and effect is unequivocal, a lesson does not have to be a traumatic experience—unless you choose for it to be. You are not here to endure hardships as far as the Will of God is concerned. You are here to meet your challenges joyfully and lovingly by transmuting all negative energies in the experience or condition. If you are not doing that, you are not fulfilling your part of the Plan.

You have the power to eliminate every negative condition in your life, and you have the power to keep your life on the right track as you evolve spiritually. Many people think that a karmic pattern of illness means that they must experience a debilitating disease, be wracked with pain, and undergo untold suffering in order to "pay for their sins" and be free of the burden. That is absolute nonsense. If you had known when you first began to experience ill health that it was nothing more than an illusion calling for your attention, simply an outpicturing of a faulty belief system and negative emotions, you could have retired to your quiet place with these kind of thoughts in your mind:

Obviously this is a signal that there is a misconception and a misunderstanding in my mind regarding the perfection of my body. I am glad that this has surfaced now so that I can eliminate these error patterns once and for all. I know that I don't have to be sick to burn away these patterns. I don't have to suffer or experience pain for the old tapes to be erased. I simply have to recognize them for what they are and rise above them in consciousness. I need only to touch the hem of the garment of my Higher Self, and I am totally healed. The permanence of the healing depends on how I choose to think and feel and act from this moment on. By being aware of the reason for my illness, I can now take the lesson and pass the test. With this understanding, I choose to break the karmic wheel by realizing that God is my health, God is my life, and God is eternally being me! Therefore, it is impossible for me to suffer ill health. I can only enjoy radiant perfection and abundant well-being.

You would continue to meditate daily on your oneness with God, forgiving everyone and everything, loving all unconditionally, choosing to express only the radiant perfection of your Christ Self, constantly accepting your wholeness in mind and body, and living each day with a sense of having a body fashioned after the perfect pattern in God-Mind. The result? Sickness would soon be so foreign to you that it would not even be a part of your consciousness. And the same would hold true for finances, personal relationships, career fulfillment, and every other aspect of your life. A "lesson" is simply a calling for forgiveness and a correction in mind.

Lessons You Have Already Learned

Karma is the law of cause and effect, which means that it does not always have a negative connotation. In your many lives, including the present one, you have also sown good thoughts, words, and deeds, and you are reaping the effects of that good work. So take an inventory of your life now to discover the lessons that you have already mastered.

You may realize that you've hardly been sick in your entire life, or that relationship problems have been few and far between, or that you have always had plenty of money to do whatever you wanted to do. Perhaps you are deeply content with your career, and feel that you have achieved a level of success that provides fulfillment in your life. We should never look at what's wrong in our evaluations without also looking at what's right, and in doing so we will usually find that the positive outweighs the negative.

Take a review of your life now, and write down the beautiful highlights in your workbook. From the vantage point of lessons learned, you may find that you are closer to the mountaintop than you thought. Ask yourself: "What's *right* with me? What are the positives in my life? Where do I feel complete and whole?" Start writing, and every time you pause, just ask again: *"What's right with me?"*

Chapter Two

◆ ◈ ◆

Your Gifts and Talents

Under the law of compensation, for every lesson to be learned in a lifetime, there is also a gift to be shared with others—a talent for you to utilize in helping others master their challenges, learn their lessons, and awaken to the Truth.

One place to look for your gifts and talents is in your astrological *rising* sign. In *The Jewel in the Lotus,* we read that the rising sign "indicates the Soul's purpose in a chart. It is far more important than the Birth Sign, or, in fact, any other single feature in the horoscope in the science of Esoteric Astrology which deals with the astrology of the Soul...."[1] And according to the Tibetan Master Djwhal Khul, "The ascendant or rising sign indicates the intended life or immediate soul purpose in this incarnation."[2]

Yes, our essential Self does have a purpose in living through the personality, and the rising sign will show that purpose—and in order to fulfill it in the most efficient manner, the Self will quicken a particular living energy within us—an angel. As I wrote in my book *Angel Energy*, "...while it is true that we can repress the energy of the angels through our ego projection, it is also true that we can never subjugate all twenty-two powers at the same time. Regardless of our state of consciousness—and no matter how guilty we may be judging ourselves over errors in thought, word, and deed—at least one of the angels is always free to love and nourish us without judgment, or to work a miracle if necessary. Even the most closed minds can't completely shut out the Light. There is always a Holy Helper available when times seem darkest."[3]

That quickened energy within us, representing a part of the Higher Self's purpose, is our gift for life. Determine your rising sign now and accept the gift, as shown below.

Rising Sign	*The Gift*
Aries	The energy of power and authority—providing determination and strong decisiveness with reliance on the Will of God.
Taurus	The energy of spiritual understanding to lift the vibration of consciousness to the level of spiritual perception.
Gemini	The energy of loving relationships—ensuring that you make the correct choice in relationships.
Cancer	The energy of victory and triumph to help you meet your objectives with determination.

Leo	The energy of spiritual strength and will—the mental will, emotional determination, and physical fortitude to follow the spiritual path.
Virgo	The energy of discernment—to help you be prudent and judicious, to take actions based on proper discernment.
Libra	The energy of order and harmony—to help you maintain balance and fairness in all situations; the peace vibration in consciousness.
Scorpio	The energy of spiritual transformation—the death and rebirth energy to help you overcome ego and realize your spiritual identity.
Sagittarius	The energy of patience and acceptance, enabling you to trust the divine process and live each day with calm equanimity.
Capricorn	The energy of spiritual grounding—also called the energy of materiality and temptation—a divine protection from the world of effects.
Aquarius	The energy of service and synthesis, motivating you to greater service to the world—all parts forming a whole.
Pisces	The energy of imagination and liberation to strengthen the spiritual vision, to image abstractly and see with the inner eye.

(For a deeper understanding of these living energies within and how they serve as special talents, I recommend my book, *The Angels Within Us.*[4])

Your gifts, talents, or characteristics of consciousness—which represent the second section in your workbook—can also be seen as positive seeds sown in the past—that is, good karma. And they must be used in the service of others if you are to receive the full benefit. As you work with your consciousness to rise above the challenges representing your karmic debts, if you will simultaneously use your gifts to the fullest service of others, the combination of the learning and serving will so greatly accelerate your progress that you will be lifetimes ahead in your spiritual evolution.

Another way to take full inventory of your gifts is to ask yourself: "What have I always wanted to do or be? What is my heart's desire? Where are my interests? What do I enjoy doing the most?" Spend several days contemplating these questions, and the answers will begin to flow into your mind. Go back to your childhood and come forward, remembering all those yearnings you've had. Write them down and see where the common denominator is. You'll find it. It may be something that you would discount or overlook because you could not see it as a means of supporting yourself in a job or career. Or it may be difficult for you to equate a particular heart's desire with a talent or gift.

For example, if you have always had the urge to travel and see faraway lands, you may think of this as something you will do after you retire, or in your later years, as strictly a leisure activity. But this may not be what Spirit has in mind. The desire to travel may be due to the "connection" you feel for people of different backgrounds and cultures—and through the gifts of love and understanding, along with respect, admiration, and a sense of brotherhood you feel, you will do your part in healing the sense of separation. Perhaps the urge to travel will be the stimulus that will cause you to investigate the travel industry, which will lead to a career opportunity, setting the stage for future trips abroad where you will fully utilize your talents in the service of God and humanity.

Based on the above example, you can see that it will be necessary to evaluate your heart's desire and see what the purpose behind it may be—because the gift is not always obvious. Or you may be fully cognizant of your gift but not know what to do with it. For greater understanding of your gift and how to use it, follow this exercise for seven days: Each morning, immediately upon awakening, ask yourself, "What do I intuitively feel my greatest strength to be? What do I intuitively feel my special gift or talent is?"

As you ask each question, write down the immediate thought that comes to mind. Do not stop to analyze or evaluate the answer—just write what comes to you. Ask the two questions and write down the answers. Once that is done, ask yourself one final question: "What do I intuitively feel my Higher Self wants me to do with these special attributes?" Again, put on paper the immediate response. Continue the process each day for seven days, not missing one single day. You will find that the answers for the first three days will be colored somewhat by your ego, but by the fourth day you will have broken through to a higher realm of consciousness, and the answers will pour forth with greater clarity.

What are some examples of gifts and talents? How about love, joy, and the ability to see something good in everything? Also, think about wisdom and understanding, and the use of these gifts to help others move through a difficult time. Consider the ability to work with children in a variety of capacities, having a sense of humor and making others laugh, and the ability to create order out of chaos through proper organization. There are musical talents, using the voice, playing various instruments, and the ability to act and create a role so real that the audience loses all sense of time and space. And what about cooking? My mother pours so much love into the preparation of food that she could make a rock taste good. Think about the ability to make something with your hands, capture beauty in a photograph, paint a picture, write a story or a poem, or teach someone—whether in a classroom or not.

There are so many additional gifts, and we have the potential to possess all of them—but certain ones are more pronounced in each individual consciousness. So find your gift—your talent—and polish it to perfection by using it to make this a better world.

Chapter Three

$\diamond \quad \diamondsuit \quad \diamond$

Your Life Program

Your Life Program—the third section in your workbook—is all that you can desire, all that you can see with your uplifted vision. The Life Program of your Divine Plan is the abundant livingness that the Father has for you now. Remember that the word *desire* means "from the Father"—so all that you desire for the life more abundant, the life more creative, the life more fulfilling, the life more loving, the life more beautiful, the life more perfect, is Spirit knocking on the door of your consciousness and saying, "It's all yours now! All that I am, you are, and all that I have is yours now. Take it! Love it! Enjoy it! This is my Divine Plan for you."

Start writing your Life Program this very day. What do you want in life? I don't mean just making a list or a treasure map. Lists and maps are fine for the manifestation of things, but we're talking about a Life Program of *experiences* now, and the experiences will include the things. This is your opportunity to write the greatest drama ever written—and it will be for *you* because it will be the drama of *your* life. At the top of the first page in this section of your workbook, write: "I see myself..." and then write what you see from the standpoint of your highest vision. The choice is totally yours: What do you want to do and be and have? Drop all the can'ts, all the inhibitions. Put yourself at the center of your world, and build around you.

As you begin to write your scenario, the first thing should be how you see yourself spiritually. For example:

> *I see myself as a spiritual being, as the very Christ of God. I am so conscious of the Christ Self within that I have become that Self. I live and move and have my being in Christ, as Christ, and I am now the Master that I was created to be.*

The second part of your script should be how you see the world, and the view of yourself living in the world:

> *I see myself living in a world of perfect peace and harmony, in a world filled with love and joy where the sense of separation from our Source is completely healed and mankind is now living as Godkind.*

Next, go back to the first section of your workbook and recall the lessons you came in to learn—and write your script showing the mastery of these lessons. For example, if it was the inability to enjoy a close, loving relationship with a soulmate, you might write something like this:

> *I see myself in a beautiful loving relationship, warm and tender, yet stimulating and exciting. I see perfect*

unconditional love in action between the two of us, and it is so beautiful. And I love the fun, the frolic, and the gaiety that I see in our relationship. We are so happy together!

Write the scenes in detail, write the dialogue between the two of you, and describe the activities with great feeling.

Now take a close look at the good seeds that you have sown in the past that are now being harvested. Remember that you have learned these lessons, but you want to enhance your mastery of them in this lifetime. So if you've enjoyed good health, do not leave this attribute out of your Life Program. You may write:

I see myself with a magnificently healthy body in perfect order, where every cell is in the image of the perfect pattern, and I am whole and complete.

The key is to put it into your own words, words that reflect your highest vision and evoke the greatest feelings of joy.

Then look at your gifts and talents, and see where you can find the deepest satisfaction in your life's work—whatever that may be. We're talking about your True Place now, where you see yourself doing what you've always wanted to do. And don't say you're too old or too young or too uneducated or too whatever. Throw away the excuses. Just write scenes showing yourself enjoying the greatest fulfillment of your eternal life—and don't be concerned with the financial part of it, or how you're going to make money doing what you really want to do. That's a separate part of your plan, so see yourself now doing what you have always wanted to do. Just write: "I see myself..." and write what you see.

Once this is complete, you can phase in the abundance of

supply in your Life Program by seeing yourself as wealthy as you want to be:

I see myself financially independent and totally secure, with lavish abundance.

Don't be concerned about where the money will come—that's none of your business. Just see yourself overflowing with abundance and attracting bountiful prosperity from every direction, and write what you see.

Develop the other scenes of your life as you see ideal and perfect fulfillment, covering every desire, mastering every challenge, learning every lesson, capitalizing on every strength, using every gift and talent, and living life to the fullest. Don't worry about your writing style, your punctuation, or perhaps your inability to create vivid and dramatic scenes. You're not writing for publication—you are writing for *you*! If you want to make changes in the script later, that's fine because it's your Life Program. The main thing you want to do now is to set the direction of your life according to your greatest desires and your highest vision. Remember, as we see ourselves, so we tend to become.

I see myself energetic, inspired, and enthusiastic. I see myself loving and loved, unconditionally. I see myself poised, confident, and filled with the power of absolute faith. I see myself as whole and complete, with an all-sufficiency of all things. I see myself with perfect judgment and as Divine Wisdom in action. I see myself as strong, mighty, and powerful. I see myself as eternal Life in perfect expression. I see myself joyous, happy, and delighted to be me. I see myself enjoying the Good Will of God every single day. I see myself with perfect under-

standing. I see myself as the Light of the world. I see myself as God being me.

Bringing your Life Program into visibility. After you have written your Life Program in detail—making sure that the scenes and visions evoke great love, joy, and excitement—go to a quiet place, sit up straight, and take several deep breaths as you focus on the Love Center in your heart. Stir up that feeling of love until you feel its magnificent vibration, then read your Life Program to yourself with great feeling. Read the Program either silently or aloud, whichever way stirs up the greatest emotion in you. "I see myself..." Read it with overflowing love. "I see myself..." Read it with joyful tears. "I see myself..." Read it with power and strength. "I see myself..." Read it with great happiness. Read each word with feeling, and lovingly contemplate the scenes that come into your mind. Take as long as necessary to establish, register, and impress your deeper-than-conscious level of mind with the details of your Program.

Once you do this, you have the pattern, the mental equivalent, the mold for your Life Program—and it will remain etched in your consciousness unless you change the pattern. And this is why it is wise to read your Life Program each day until the manifestation occurs.

After the pattern is established, it is up to the power, the substance, the creative energy of Spirit to give it form and experience. And while Infinite Mind is going to be the primary actor on stage now, you still have a vital role to play in the co-creation, as follows:

1. First, remember who you are. The Reality of you is pure Spirit, the very Christ of God, the Lord-God-Self that you are in Truth.

2. Secondly, understand that the Life Program you create in your mind and write in words is not your conception. It is from your Higher Self; it is how your God-Self wants to express in your world. So you can relax, knowing that you don't have to make anything happen. All you have to do is take the blueprint into consciousness to establish the pattern.

3. Thirdly, the creative energy of that Infinite Mind within you is the substance of every form and experience of your Life Program. That radiant energy—that overflowing substance—is forever pouring, radiating from the Supermind within, right through your consciousness and out into the physical world to become all that you desire. As it moves through the pattern of your Life Program, the energy takes on the attributes of the program and begins to materialize them by changing its rate of vibration.

4. The fourth point in the co-creation process: If you keep your focus on the *forms* of your Life Program, your mind will tell you after a time that there are not enough opportunities to meet the right mate, not enough money to accomplish your goals, not enough contacts to find your true place, not enough physical well-being to meet your objectives, not enough time to do all that you want to do, not enough of whatever. And the reason is because your mind will be vibrating at too low a level; your mental vibrations will have dropped so low that the manifestation cannot be completed. This is why you must keep your mind on the spiritual I AM within, knowing that God is the very substance and activity of your Life Program. And since there is never any lack of substance of God or the activity of God, there cannot be any obstacles to the fulfillment of your Program.

In other words, there is always plenty of God! When your mind begins to understand the true meaning of *omnipresence*, it beings to vibrate to a consciousness of *plenty*, and that high vibration is the one that will bring your Life Program into visibility. You should understand that your Program, which will come forth into visibility as form and experience, will be an effect of your consciousness. And you know that when you concentrate on the effect, you are forgetting the Cause, and when you do that, you are shutting down the power. You must look to God and Spirit alone as the Source of your Life Program and take your mind completely off the outer world.

In essence, when you concentrate on the effects of your world, you are lowering the vibration of your consciousness, and the lower the vibration, the more difficult it is for your good to come forth into manifestation. But when you concentrate on the Spirit-Substance of the Great I AM within you, you are raising the vibration of your consciousness. Think about this: While your mind *could* possibly conceive of a limitation of the form, it certainly could not possibly conceive of any limitation in Spirit.

Do you see now your role in the scheme of things? As a co-creator, you take your heart's desires that Spirit has given you and write the scenario for your life according to your highest vision. The Life Program of your Divine Plan is what you really want to do and be and have in your life. You give this Life Program to your consciousness with great feeling and joyful emotion so that the perfect pattern can be developed. You read the program daily to protect the pattern. At all other times, you maintain the highest possible vibration by keeping your mind on the idea that Spirit is omnipresent, that Spirit is appearing as your Life Program, that there is always plenty of Spirit; therefore, there can be no limitations involving your Life Program.

Saturate yourself with the idea of *plenty*, and the vibration of plenty will manifest in your affairs—plenty of love, plenty of health, plenty of true place opportunities, plenty of money, plenty of time, plenty of wisdom, plenty of fun, plenty of peace, plenty of joy, plenty of vitality, plenty of inspiration, PLENTY-PLENTY-PLENTY!

The Divine Plan and True Place

By way of summarizing the concept of the Divine Plan—and to give you a broader perspective of the relationship of True Place within the Plan—I'll share with you what Jason Andrews has to say on the subject. (Jason Andrews is the name used to identify an evolved Soul quoted at length in Chapter Three of *The Superbeings.*[1])

> **Andrews:** Each man, each woman, came into physical form with a purpose, a mission. Consider people living now in America, the European countries, Russia, the Far East, throughout the world. Regardless of what you may call their lot in life, each was granted entrance into the manifest world to express a particular idea, faculty, a certain level of consciousness, if you will. Never forget the uniqueness of each individual. No two are alike. Take away the mask of human identity, move past the gaze of awareness that is fastened to the illusionary world, progress on through the cave of memory, and you begin to see the soft rays of a light. The closer you approach the light, the brighter it seems. This is the Light of Reality, the point where the Universal is forever becoming the Individual. It is the pressing out of God-Mind into a particular manifestation. Here, in this secret place of the Superconsciousness, is where Uniqueness is born. God never creates identically.

At the time of the separation when man fell away from spiritual consciousness—referring to "time" figuratively, God etched deeply in each Soul a Divine Plan for reuniting Sonship. You may say that there is a Master Plan, and that each individual plan is some part of the whole, and true place symbolizes the outer expression of that inner plan. Would you not agree that true place is the special and specific activity of each individual in showing his brothers and sisters the way of At-One-Ment? Can you not see that true place is how and where you spread spiritual light?

The sharing of spiritual understanding is the cornerstone of true place, but included in this structure is life itself: the right work, the right relationships, a peaceful mind and joyful heart, and a splendid feeling of fulfillment. The Divine Plan etched in your Soul is indispensable to the whole, to the universe, for there could not be completeness without it, without you, without each individual man and woman. All parts are indispensable to the whole, therefore every Soul is equally important to God, for His idea of the Son cannot be complete without the participating unity of all the parts. Can you see now that the drunk in the gutter is as important in God's eyes as the ruler of a nation? There is no such thing as a lost soul, for every Soul is a Page in the Master Plan.

True Place is how and where you are expressing the Divine Plan for your eternal life. True Place is the effect; the Plan is the cause. Pick a stranger out of the crowd. Think how special he is. Within his Soul is a link in a universal chain of Sonship, and without that particular individual, that particular link, God's perfect idea of Himself would not be complete.

The link represents the individual's Divine Plan. If we could go within his consciousness to read his Plan, we would see a particular gift, a special talent, for providing a useful service to others. He may not have discovered this talent as yet, but it is there. There is also a magnetic force that if followed, will lead him to the geographical location on Earth where his talent may be used most effectively. This same force will also attract the right people into his life. The idea of dedicating his life to the love of God and his fellow man is there, along with infinite opportunities to give and share spiritual understanding through his thoughts, words, and deeds. Written in the Plan is the instruction to put more into the world than he takes out, to be a giver rather than a taker in consciousness. He will find the idea that his abundance is not dependent on persons or conditions, and wholeness of body is included as the perfect body idea.

As the Divine Plan comes forth to manifest as true place, he will find great fulfillment in his life's work, and will meet his responsibilities with joy and enthusiasm. The Golden Rule will be practiced in all his relationships, and order and harmony will be evident in every area of his life. He will feel complete, whole, total—spiritually, emotionally, mentally, physically. And his world will reflect this perfect balance.

Your true place is the activity of livingness. If you cannot feel this activity taking place in your life, you must take an inventory of consciousness. To do this, look at your world. Look at your life. If it is not whole and complete, you are out of alignment with your Divine Plan. You are not on the mark. To be on the mark, you must be in your place in the universe. If you are off the mark, you are out of place.

Also take inventory from within. What is your most compelling desire in your work life? Has there been an inner urging, a yearning of the heart for a change? Do not resist change. At the same time, use discernment, good judgment. Follow the calling but use wisdom. God has charted the course, and He will lead you across the river of change at the shallow point. Or He may push you off into deep water, but will support you safely across, protecting you from the currents of race-mind fears. Simply follow the inner guidance, your intuition, with confidence and peace.

Yes, a person may feel out of place in a particular job or in a particular community. If the discontent persists, meaning that it is not merely a mood or whim, he is being alerted to listen within. But the guidance, the instruction, must always be received on a consciousness of love. Otherwise the guidance may be misinterpreted, and he may take action prematurely. He must love from the heart, pouring out the energy of love to all without exception. Love will open the divine channel of communication by dissolving the fear that had clogged it. Without a consciousness of love, a person will not find true place.

In his consciousness of love, he must follow the inner guidance to the letter, not analyzing the instructions, just following them. Take action! If he waits to evaluate, and procrastinates, the entire chain of events that had been established for him will break apart. He will have missed the train, so to speak, and while another will be forthcoming, why should he wait for God's richest blessings?

Question: What if a person does not know what he wants to do—he just knows he doesn't like what he is doing?

Andrews: It doesn't matter what he wants to do. His God-Self knows what He wants to do, and that is all that is important. An individual's Divine Plan, expressing as true place, is a part of the *whole* Plan to heal the separation. To reunite the Consciousness of Sonship, each man and woman must be in a position to evolve in consciousness. To evolve in consciousness, one must be in proper alignment with the universe. The Spirit within you knows precisely where this Circle of Light is, and will make the path straight before you. Even more, He will take you there.

The Circle of Light, the Divine Plan in expression, will

give you the opportunity to grow with ease. If you are outside the Circle, you will grow with adversity. The choice is yours, but you will evolve one way or another because the Light of At-One-Ment cannot be held back.

Your work within the Circle may not be a job or career as those words are commonly defined. But whatever your role, assignment, responsibility may be, it will be an opportunity to use your particular talents in the service of others. An individual may also feel that if he or she truly loves the work that fulfills a heart's desire, the compensation for that service may be below the level of financial freedom. Ask yourself: Where is that person focusing his or her attention? God is the only source of supply, of abundance, but by looking at the job as the source, other channels will be closed. Just remember this: The Divine Plan for each individual includes successful service, abundant supply, ideal relationships, and radiant health, all in a divine atmosphere of peace, love, joy, fulfillment, and freedom.

Question: What must we do, individually, to bring the Divine Plan for our lives into manifestation?

Andrews: Give more where you are. Dedicate yourself to the job at hand, and meet each responsibility with joyful enthusiasm. Throw yourself into life by serving God and your fellow beings to the very best of your abilities. When you give more, you love more, and the more you love, the more you give. This is working with the Law, and never forget that the activity of the Law depends on two commandments that Jesus gave us: "You shall love the Lord your God with all your heart, and with all your soul, and with all your mind." This is the great and first Commandment. And a second is like it: "You shall love your neighbor as yourself." On these two commandments depend all the law and the prophets.

Has it not occurred to you what the Divine Plan is? The

Divine Plan for your life is the Christ indwelling, your spiritual nature, your Superconsciousness, your *Lord*. You cannot separate Mind from the activity of Mind. The divine ideas representing the Plan for your life are in the thought realm of your spiritual consciousness. This is the Christ of you seeing Himself in expression. When you put on Christ through the love of Christ and your fellow man, your neighbor, you are embodying the expression. When you realize your true Identity, that Identity manifests Itself through you as your true place.

It is impossible to be "in place" spiritually and be out of place in your world. You cannot be spiritually rich and materially poor. You cannot be spiritually well and suffer ill health. You cannot be the Love of Spirit in expression and experience inharmonious relationships.

The answer? The Light of God within you, your True Self, is the answer. Touch that through daily prayer and meditation. Affirm with faith and feeling that Christ in you is now made manifest in your heart, in your mind, in your body, in your affairs. Speak the word that you are now in your true place according to the Divine Plan that has been lovingly created especially for you.

In a consciousness of love, work with the Law, and easily and beautifully you will be led to the Circle of Light where your Kingdom is now in expression on Earth, as it is in Heaven.

We Are Ready for the Next Course

From our work in Part I—*The Divine Plan*—the full scope of our mission is now coming into view, and we are eager to step out on the stage of this world as the master we were created to be. This leads us to Part II of this book—*Know Thyself*—to strengthen that realization and understanding of who and what we are.

Rather than select those chapters that relate to a seeming challenge in life, it is suggested that you read Chapters Four through Seventeen in sequence and work with the Spiritual Activity for each lesson until you feel an inner acknowledgment of deeper understanding. Then begin to practice and live the principles in your daily life. And remember, no other "human" can show you a shortcut to the mountaintop. There can only be one Guide, one Teacher, one Master in your life—and that is the Divine Reality within you, your Spiritual Self. The exercises in Part II are simply to help you realize that Self as the fulfillment of every desire, the answer to every need, the solution to every problem.

PART II

KNOW THYSELF

"Be not conformed to this world but be ye transformed through the renewing of your mind..."
— St. Paul

Chapter Four

$\diamond$ $\diamond$ $\diamond$

Your Personal World

What is included in your world? Start with your body—the most immediate visible form—and move out to encompass your family, your dwelling place and the environment in which you live, your job or career, your income and possessions, the people with whom you work, your friends and social activities, and your community.

What you are seeing in this inventory of "your personal world" are *ideas* in your consciousness expressed on the third-dimensional plane. They are *your* images—and each image is nothing more or less than your finite beliefs projected into materiality. Every person in your life is there by law of consciousness, and you are sharing mental or physical space with them through either positive or negative attraction. Even your children chose you based on the state of your consciousness.

Everything comes to you or is repelled from you based on the vibration of your energy field, and the vibration is established by your beliefs and convictions. Accordingly, you can see that nothing is out of place or out of order in your life. Everything is perfect based on your consciousness and the outworking of the law. Your world is a mirror of your thoughts, feelings, and concepts—all pressed out in material form and experience.

Do you like what you see? You are the architect and the builder, and you have designed and produced your world to the exact specifications of your consciousness. Even if you became a "health nut" to achieve a healthier body—and then ran away from your spouse, home, job, friends, and present lifestyle with the idea of starting all over again in a new city or country, in time your consciousness would create an almost exact duplication of your former world. You simply cannot run away from your world, because you can't run away from yourself. You can't even escape by destroying your body, because you take your consciousness with you.

To run around trying to fix your world with the consciousness that produced the problem in the first place will only aggravate the situation even more. To change your world, you must change your consciousness. You must draw forth from within a new awareness, understanding, and knowledge of the universe, the power that sustains you, and the true nature of yourself. And with each degree in the shift in your consciousness, more Reality is revealed in your world.

Think of it this way: What you are experiencing in life are your finite ideas projected into materiality. However, behind what you see is what Spirit sees, and that Infinite Vision constitutes the Reality. For example, Spirit sees only a radiantly healthy body; therefore, the perfect body form is the only Reality, and as your consciousness becomes more in tune with Spirit, your body will change to reflect the higher Vision.

The same is true for *everything* in your life, in your world.

The infinite Perfection forever lives behind the finite conception. Behind the illusion is always the Reality.

Look at your relationships. There may be strain, turmoil, and friction from your perspective, but from the Higher Vision there is only love, harmony, and peace. How do you restore or harmonize a relationship? You don't have to do anything about the other person. The only person you have to do anything about is yourself. Through meditation and spiritual treatment, you become one with the inner Reality and let the illusion of discord fade away.

What about money? In and around and through your financial affairs is the Truth of lavish abundance—the High Vision of all-sufficiency—overflowing supply to meet every need with plenty to spare and share. If you are seeing lack, limitation, and insufficiency, you are looking at the illusion. But as the vibration of your consciousness becomes more spiritual—and you understand that the Spirit within you is appearing as your supply—the shadows of scarcity will dissolve.

Even your home and automobile are but your conceptions of a place to live and a means of transportation. Do they represent the expression of the Higher Consciousness? Is there beauty, ease, bountiful accommodations, harmony, and total dependability? Through your oneness with your Spirit, illusory restrictions will be removed. And while the "form" of the house or car will still be finite materiality, the *experience* of joyful living and happy motoring will be Spirit appearing as the new Reality.

The great majority of people on the planet see only the world of illusion because they are living out of the lower vibrations and negative energies of the ego. What is illusion? Consider illness, suffering, lack, limitation, poverty, hunger, unemployment, conflict, crime, war, accidents, and death. How can we call these seemingly real experiences illusions? Because they are not the Will of God—and only that which is the Cosmic Urge expressed is real.

How do you move from illusion to Reality? By awakening to your True Nature, by becoming of one accord with the Higher Self and *letting* that Self appear as every needed thing or experience in your life. As you realize your oneness with the Spirit of God within, your personal world will change dramatically; your pocket of materiality on Earth will take on a new vibration—one that reflects the Higher Vision. You will have co-created a new Garden, and the Light from your Garden will be a harmonizing influence for the rest of the world.

Spiritual Activity

Make a list in your workbook of everything you consider to be a part of "your" world. Include the people around you, your place of employment—and the experiences, situations, and conditions where you exert influence and where you feel the influence of others. After your list is complete, review it with this thought in mind:

> *My world is simply my consciousness projected on the screen of life, and anything I see that is not in perfect harmony is not the Will of God; therefore, it is not real.*

Next, take the individual parts of your world—that is, your body, relationships, finances, job, and so on, and contemplate each one separately. As you do, begin to see in your mind's eye and feel in your heart that God's Vision of Reality—of *Truth*—is in, around, and through that particular phase of your life. See it as radiant light filling the entire condition or situation, and know that this Activity of God is the Divine Will in expression.

Spend several minutes at various times throughout the day contemplating that glorious Reality of total fulfillment, knowing that as you lift up your consciousness—your vision—you will be working with the Law in totally transforming your personal world.

Chapter Five

❖ ❖ ❖

The Christ Connection

Y ou are always expressing the idea of who and what you are.
If you think of yourself as a human being, you are going to
experience that identity. But when you take the Idea that you are
a spiritual being, that you are God individualized, and begin to
live that Idea every moment of every day, your entire world
begins to take on a different tone and shape.

Look at the Idea again in different words:

> *The Identity of God is individualized as me now. I am
> the Self-Expression of God. I am the Presence of God
> where I am. I am the Christ of God.*

This is the *Christ Idea* we are talking about—and it is this
Idea that will help you to rise above the twists and turns and tri-
als and tribulations of humanhood. Your human consciousness
must begin using the Christ Idea if it is to be transformed back to

its original state of perfection.

To conceive and live the Idea that you are God in expression, with all the powers of God at your disposal, is to "plant your consciousness in spirituality." When you take the Christ Idea, you are not just putting on a mask and playing make-believe. A mask is a disguise, a cover-up. What you are doing is revealing Reality. Remember that your whole consciousness once knew itself to be God made manifest, and even when you were enveloped in sense consciousness, your Spirit remained free and is right now concentrated in a Love Vibration within your energy field.

Another point of vital importance: Right within the darkened part of your lower-vibration mind, buried beneath layers of sense consciousness, is a *memory*, a faint mental impression of all that you once were. Now think of it. When you say "I am God's perfect expression; God is as me now"—you are refreshing your memory. You are agreeing with something that you already know.

When you formulate this Master Idea of Who and What you are, the Idea first enters your intellectual awareness, then moves into the feeling nature (subconscious) and quickly attaches itself to it—and that ancient memory is stimulated and its dawning begins to illumine your conscious mind with new understanding.

When you first begin to understand Who and What you are, it is much like the Prodigal Son who "came to himself." Your memory has been stirred, and the awakening process has begun. As the awakening deepens and expands in your thinking and feeling natures, a new vibration forms in consciousness. The energy of the Christ Idea begins to think and to know itself as a Divine Idea, an Idea related to your Self, your Superconsciousness. And so the Christ Idea says to itself, "I will arise and go to my father." Its vibration begins to move through the inner space of consciousness, through the walls and layers of erroneous thoughts and false beliefs, through levels of hardened patterns of fear and doubt.

When the Christ Idea is still far from home, the Soul of Reality within, the Christ Truth, sees it and begins moving toward it. "But when he was yet a great way off, his father saw him and had compassion, and ran and fell on his neck and kissed him." This means that as the Christ Idea begins to move through consciousness toward the Reality within, your Holy Self begins to radiate and move toward the Divine Idea. The "kiss" is the union of human consciousness expressing as the Christ Idea, and your Divine Consciousness. This is the Realization. This is the Experience. At that glorious moment, the merging Lights become one, and your being is filled with the Light of Truth. You are born anew.

Do you see how your Identity-Idea can change your life? It changes the way you think, feel, and act—and literally transforms your consciousness. When that mystical union with Self takes place, you become "Christed"—and all the powers of God come forth in a Master Mind Consciousness, and you live under the Law of Grace. But you do not have to wait for Christhood to begin experiencing harmony in your affairs. While the Christ Idea is making its journey home across the planes of inner consciousness, the spiritual law of cause and effect will be working *for* you.

In effect, this Law says to you: "Whatever you conceive yourself to be, I will outpicture in your life and affairs. If your mind fluctuates between Godhood and humanhood, I will reflect that vacillation in your world. However, as you live the Idea that *God is as me now* with great joy, love, enthusiasm, and dedication—as you fill your mind and heart with this Divine Idea—I will work effortlessly to bring forth in your life all that this Idea represents. Then when the Experience comes and you begin to live under Grace, everything in your life will be a direct reflection of the Christ Truth."

Until the Experience, until the Realization, the Christ Idea *is* the Christ Indwelling. It represents the Divine Potential. It is the Christ Child born in the stable of your lower mind: "Unto us a child is born, unto us a son is given, and the government shall be upon his shoulder." And the governing of your life *will* be upon his shoulder because the Christ Idea will be directing the Law, sending it before you to straighten out every crooked place.

"...and his name shall be called Wonderful, Counsellor, the mighty God, the everlasting Father, the Prince of Peace." How can an *Idea* be given these holy attributes of God? Think about it for a moment. The Law says that whatever you hold in consciousness will be outpictured in your world. Accordingly, the Christ Idea held in consciousness will heal your body, prosper your affairs, and restore your relationships. Would you not call this Wonderful?

The Christ Idea symbolizes infinite Intelligence, so the Law will interpret this Knowingness for you and will direct and govern your affairs. Could you ask for a better Counselor? "Mighty God" means power, and the Law working through and as the Divine Idea in consciousness is omnipotent. There is nothing it cannot do for you.

The "everlasting Father" is representative of Divine Love, and the Law, working through this aspect of the Christ Idea, will smooth out every difficulty and attract love to you in full measure. As the "Prince of Peace," the Christ Idea will quiet your mind, still your emotions, and bring forth a sense of peace that passeth all understanding. The Christ Idea is the Christ Child who will overcome the world, *your* world, and "of the increase of His government and peace there shall be no end...."

Spiritual Activity

Spend from 10 to 15 minutes today—in two separate sessions—contemplating the thoughts below. Immediately following the meditation periods, listen within and write in your workbook the related ideas that come to you.

- *God is right where I am, and I am eternally aware of this Presence. God conceived within Its Mind an Idea of Itself in expression. I am that Idea made manifest. God is expressing as me now. I am the expression of God. I am the Christ.*

- *The Law, the creative energy of God-Mind, is flowing through the Idea that I am now living. That Idea is the Christ, the Self-expression of God that I am, and my world becomes a reflection of that Idea.*

- *As Christ is the Healing Principle, so the Law restores my body according to the Perfect Pattern.*

- *As Christ is the Abundance Principle, an all-sufficiency of supply now manifests for my use.*

- *As Christ is the Harmony Principle, all of my relationships are lovingly renewed and strengthened.*

- *I am now the Living Truth of Wholeness and Fulfillment.*

CHAPTER SIX

◆ ◈ ◆

NO MAN'S LAND

As you move through the inner space of consciousness toward the union with Self, there is a bridge you must pass over. It is the link between the third and fourth dimensions, and it is on this bridge that you shed the remaining particles of error thoughts and negative beliefs and go through the final cleansing. It has been called "no man's land" because it is the point of separating with the ego just before uniting with the Total Self in consciousness.

As the bridge comes into view, your world may seem to turn upside down, and the reason is that you are beginning the process of letting go of everything that seemed secure to you in the three-dimensional world. Depending on the degree of your functioning in lower mind vibrations, your ego may choose to do battle as you step on to the bridge, and it will do whatever is necessary to save itself.

If that means creating an insufficiency of funds, it will do it, because this effect could very well cause you to step back into the old ways of thinking and assume personal control of the situation, which would put the ego back on the throne of the mental world. Another ego tantrum may give the appearance of a business failure, or the interruption of a successful career, or perhaps a physical ailment. The ego simply wants to show who is boss.

Throughout the world, men and women are moving up in consciousness and are reaching the higher realms, and as they close in on the borderland of the Kingdom, the ego starts to panic. It knows that when the bridge is crossed, its role in the scheme of things will be reduced from master to servant.

But remember the story of the Prodigal Son again. As you step out on the bridge, the Christ within, the very Spirit of God, comes forth to meet you—and this Omnipotent Presence will meet you at the halfway point. You don't have to make the journey across no man's land alone. You only have to go halfway, and at this center point you are engulfed in the Light and are taken into the Spiritual Dimension with the everlasting arms of Love around you.

How do you navigate the last mile as the ego begins to fight for its life? You totally surrender to God. You literally take on an "I don't care" attitude—regardless of what is going on in the world around you. You turn everything in your life over to the Christ within and give up all concern, knowing that your God-Self is the solution to every problem and the answer to every need, and that Spirit cannot let you down because it is against God's nature to do so!

In "The Manifestation Process" from my book *Empowerment*,[1] I point out that we know when we have truly surrendered by "the total lack of concern, anxiety, and outside pressure in our consciousness. This negative energy will have been replaced with the positive vibrations of peace, joy, and confidence...." Of course, surrendering and reaching this state of mind is sometimes easier said than done, because even as you begin to give up to the Higher Power, the ego will do what it can to bring you out on the battlefield again.

Total surrender means to not resist, attack, or fear anything. It means to have the courage, perhaps for the first time in your life, to put your trust in God and only God. It means to place your faith in Omnipotence and not in the potential actions of your creditors, to trust the Activity of Spirit and not the illusory activities of this world, to believe in the One Cause rather than in negative appearances.

If checks are bouncing, creditors are calling, your business is failing, your spouse has left, the children have turned savage, and your body seems to be falling apart, what is the worst thing that can happen? You cannot die. You are not going to be eaten alive. You cannot really lose anything because all material effects can be recreated. And the only person you can do anything about is yourself. So what are you afraid of? If you say anything other than "nothing," it's the ego talking.

When you get to the end of your rope, let go. Underneath are the Everlasting Arms. God is your support! Remember the promise: "For I, Jehovah thy God, will hold thy right hand, saying unto thee, Fear not; I will help thee." God is your security! "I will fear no evil for thou art with me." When you turn away from the illusions of this world and completely surrender your life and affairs to the infinite Love, Wisdom, Power, and Activity of Spirit, the ego is smothered by the blanket of spiritual Light that enters your consciousness. And you are free to complete your journey home, knowing that God will meet you halfway.

Spiritual Activity

Read and meditate on these promises from the Psalms.

Psalm 27:

The Lord is my light and my salvation; whom shall I fear? The Lord is the strength of my life; of whom shall I be afraid?

When the wicked, even my enemies and my foes, came upon me to eat up my flesh, they stumbled and fell.

Though a host should encamp against me, my heart shall not fear: though war should rise against me, in this will I be confident.

One thing have I desired of the Lord, that will I seek after; that I may dwell in the house of the Lord all the days of my life, to behold the beauty of the Lord, and to enquire in his temple.

For in the time of trouble he shall hide me in his pavilion: in the secret of his tabernacle shall he hide me; he shall set me up upon a rock.

And now shall mine head be lifted up above mine enemies round about me: therefore will I offer in his tabernacle sacrifices of joy; I will sing, yea, I will sing praises unto the Lord.

Psalm 91:

He that dwelleth in the secret place of the most High shall abide under the shadow of the Almighty.

I will say of the Lord, He is my refuge and my fortress: my God; in him will I trust.

Surely he shall deliver thee from the snare of the fowler, and from the noisome pestilence.

He shall cover thee with his feathers, and under his wings shall thou trust: his truth shall be thy shield and buckler.

Thou shalt not be afraid for the terror by night; nor for the arrow that flieth by day;

Nor for the pestilence that walketh in darkness; nor for the destruction that wasteth at noonday.

A thousand shall fall at thy side, and ten thousand at thy right hand; but it shall not come nigh thee.

Only with thine eyes shalt thou behold and see the reward of the wicked.

Because thou hast made the Lord, which is my refuge, even the most High, thy habitation;

There shall no evil befall thee, neither shall any plague come nigh thy dwelling.

For he shall give his angels charge over thee, to keep thee in all thy ways.

They shall bear thee up in their hands, lest thou dash thy foot against a stone.

Thou shalt tread upon the lion and adder: the young lion and the dragon shalt thou trample under feet.

Because he hath set his love upon me, therefore will I deliver him: I will set him on high, because he hath known my name.

He shall call upon me, and I will answer him: I will be with him in trouble; I will deliver him, and honor him.

With long life will I satisfy him, and show him my salvation.

CHAPTER SEVEN

❖ ❖ ❖

THE CHOICE IS YOURS

Some people feel that it is spiritually wrong to desire any-thing—and a few metaphysical writers follow the theme of "desireless living" in their books. They are basing this concept on Jesus' instructions to "Take no thought for your life...your Father knoweth that ye have need of these things. But rather seek ye the kingdom of God; and all these things shall be added unto you." (Luke 12:22-32)

To understand the meaning behind this instruction, we have to look at it from two different levels of consciousness. The first level is predominantly "human" in that the full robe of spiritual consciousness has not been put on. On this level, we work spiritually to uplift and expand consciousness, but at the same time we are given the opportunity to shape and mold our world through the use of the various power centers established within our consciousness. We have the power of free will to determine what we want in life, and we have the authority to call forth our good through the powers of the spoken word, imagination, enthusiasm, joy, and faith. And then we *release* our desires, our needs, to the higher Vision and Power of the Christ Self within, and we give no further thought to the concept of NEED.

As I stated in the Preface to *The Superbeings*, "The key thought that came forth from within went something like this: 'Claim your good. Imagine your good. Speak the word for your good. Then care not if your good ever comes to pass.' That seemed to be quite a contradiction at first. If I desired something with all my heart, I did care if the desire was fulfilled or not. But that caring, which is another word for worry and concern, was actually diverting the power flow. I was told to choose what I wanted, see it as an actuality, call it forth into visible form and experience—then not be concerned about the outcome regardless of how desperate the need."[1] In other words, *take no thought*. Let it go, release it, turn it over to the Higher Power, and get out of the way of the marvelous creative activity of Spirit.

Now let's move up to a higher level of consciousness and see what it means to "take no thought." Simply stated, when your consciousness of Truth is the ruling force in your mental and emotional natures, this consciousness will automatically be reflected or outpictured in your world and affairs without any concentrated effort (thought) on your part. This is what it means to live under grace, as a beholder of God in action through you. And this is our objective, our ultimate goal, but until we reach that level of consciousness, let's use the faculties, the powers, the living energies, and the attributes we have at our disposal—one of which is the ability to *choose*.

Pause for a moment now and look at your life. Are you experiencing any kind of lack or limitation? Are you suffering from any type of physical ailment? Is your work boring and unfulfilling? Whether you answered "yes" or "no" is not the point; the point is that you are simply experiencing that which you have already chosen. Think of it this way: You could not have lack, sickness, unfulfillment, and strained relationships unless you first chose these particular experiences in your life. How can this be? You cannot have anything in life—positive or negative—unless you *accept* it, and you cannot accept it unless you make up your mind to do so, and when you make up your mind about anything, that is the action of *choosing.*

It should be obvious to you now that you are constantly choosing every moment of every day, so isn't it time to start choosing rightly? Isn't today the day to start acting rather than reacting? As you are sitting and reading this book, why not make a firm decision in your mind to do what you want to do, be what you want to be, and have what you want to have. Begin now to take control of your mind and emotions, and to focus on the peace, joy, love, abundance, and radiant perfection that have always been yours. *On this day, choose that which you desire!*

Spiritual Activity

If you have completed the Life Program section in your workbook, go back and review the story that you have written about your life. If you have not begun this phase of your Divine Plan, you are encouraged to do so at once. Choose the experiences and activities that will be a part of your life beginning this day. Stake your claim to *all* your good—then release everything to Spirit and relax. Let go and let God be God. And remember, take no thought as to how your good is to come about. "God works in mysterious ways His wonders to perform"..."My ways are ingenious, my methods are sure"..."Trust in me, commit your ways unto me."

CHAPTER EIGHT

THE ALL-IN-ALL OF SELF

You always receive according to what you recognize your True Self to be. One day in meditation I was told: "That which you believe I am, I AM." In other words, whatever your consciousness attributes to your God-Self will determine your demonstration. If you believe the Spirit within to be the life and health of your body, then this perfection will be outpictured in your body. If you believe that your Master Self is your supply, you will never be at a loss for money. This is the key: You must be aware that whatever you seek in life, you already have—because your Higher Self *is* it. Whatever fulfillment you associate with your Self will be yours. So if you want to demonstrate radiant health, gain the consciousness that your True Self *is* your health. If you want more financial abundance in your life, gain the consciousness that your Self *is* your abundance, *is* your prosperity. When you achieve a consciousness of your inner Self as the All-in- All, the Giver and the Gift, you will be stepping up to mastery.

In my experience, I have found that I could pray and affirm and visualize and speak the word for days on end without anything happening—because I was trying to make something happen. Only when I went within and *let* my God-Self enter my awareness—to where I could truly say "I AM" from a sense of spiritual identity—did my world begin to change. And I have realized that it is my consciousness of God *as* the needed thing or experience that causes the change, and the greater and deeper the consciousness, the more dramatic and rapid the change.

Your awareness, understanding, and knowledge must be based on the Truth that God, as your All-in-All, is right where you are, individualized as you, appearing as you. This means that you do not have to go far to find the Whole Spirit of God. You only have to take your mind off the illusions of "this world" and turn within in contemplative meditation. Very soon you will sense an infinite Knowingness, and your emotional nature will tingle with warmth and love. As you continue on the inner journey, the whole vibration of your being changes and you become a transparency for the Light. Now Spirit is released to go before you to "make all things new."

But sometimes before your world becomes a reflection of this inner Perfection, you shut the door to Spirit and take over the controls once again. So whether you have a total adjustment in your life depends on how long you can keep the door open, how long you can allow the Master Consciousness within to work before the little self jumps in and says "my turn." That's the ego getting in the way.

Until there is a full realization and consciousness "locks in" to the Christ Vibration, you must watch your every step. It is much like balancing a jug on your head. When you keep your mind on the Presence within, you are in balance. But if you take your mind off the inner realm of Spirit and place the focus on the world of effect, the slightest stumble in consciousness will topple the jug, and you may have a few shattered prayers. The problem is mental laziness. It comes down to a matter of priority.

When we look at the priority system of many of the evolved ones, we see that it is quite different from those still operating out of the lower consciousness. Most began with dedication and commitment, saying in effect: "I refuse to accept anything but perfect harmony in my life. I will not be sick, I will not be poor, I will not accept inharmonious relationships, and through the Spirit of God I AM, I will shatter these illusions and build a new model of Reality—a new world of peace, joy, abundance, wellness, loving relationships, true place success, fulfillment—a heaven on earth." And so they established the priority of achieving mastery over this world, and they never lost sight of this goal. Many even made a covenant with God, written, dated, and signed.

Are you ready to take your vows to achieve mastery? This does not mean that you have to withdraw from the world and live like a monk. It means that you begin to really *live* life as the delightful child of God you are in Truth. And your covenant with the Spirit within does not have to sound like an agreement written by a team of corporate attorneys. Make it simple, but make it meaningful—and I will assure you that if you will keep your part of the agreement, you will marvel at the miracles taking place in your life.

Write your covenant according to the dictates of your heart. Here is an example that may help you:

> *I agree from this moment on to do my very best to keep my mind on the Presence within, to feel love and joy, to think loving thoughts toward all, and to always act from a sense of inward direction. To accomplish this, I*

now release all fears, concerns, resentment, condemna-tion, and unforgiveness. I surrender all past mistakes and errors in judgment, and I empty out all false pride and ego-centered emotions. Everything in my consciousness that could possibly hold me in bondage I now cast upon the Christ within to be dissolved. I now choose to live under grace, to be the perfect open channel through which Divine Love, Wisdom, and Power flow forth as the Activity of Spirit in my life. And I see and know this Activity to be the perfect harmonizing of all relation-ships, the perfect adjustment in all situations, the perfect release from all entanglements, the perfect supply for abundant living, the perfect health of my body, the per-fect fulfillment in my life. I now go forth in faith, putting my trust in the Christ within, and living each moment with a heart overflowing with gratitude, love, and joy.

You keep your part of the agreement by thinking, feeling, speaking, and acting in accordance with what you have written. And you practice the Presence throughout each day—seeing yourself as God in expression, affirming that the Master Consciousness indwelling is now appearing as your all-sufficiency, seeing your good from your highest vision, and speaking the word that the activity of Spirit is the only power at work in your life.

Remember that you must not only practice the Presence (see the Christ) in yourself, but in all others, too. Understand that there is only one Self in all the universe, one Selfhood—and this Selfhood appears as you, as me, as each individual. Therefore, each and every Soul throughout the universe is a spiritual being—and since my I AM is your I AM, whatever I am saying about you I am saying about me. If I criticize you, I am criticizing myself. If

I see you as poor and weak and unfulfilled, I am seeing myself as poor and weak and unfulfilled. And what I see or say about myself is conditioning my consciousness accordingly.

Because of the way the Law works, if I believe that you are suffering from any kind of lack, I am calling for an experience of lack in my life. If I judge by appearances that you are ill, I am setting up the possibility for illness to manifest in my body. Now do you understand why we must not judge others—and why it is absolutely imperative to love thy neighbor as thyself?

Spiritual Activity

Whenever a "need" comes to your mind, identify it consciously and then turn within and recognize that your Higher Self is the immediate answer. Begin to associate everything that you could possibly desire in the outer world with Spirit within as total fulfillment. This shift in focus from effect to Cause will help to clear the channel for the activity of Spirit. Remember, the power can work for you only as it works through you. For example:

If you need or desire:	Contemplate Spirit appearing as:
Money	Lavish abundance, an all-sufficiency of supply with a divine surplus.
Wellness	The restoring Power in every cell and organ, the pure and holy Life of the body; energy, vitality, and wholeness.

A loving relationship

The way, means, circumstance and situation for the attraction of the right person, at the right time and right place, the drawing together of souls in an ideal relationship.

To heal a relationship

The energy of Unconditional Love joyously healing and harmonizing the situation.

A job

The perfect opportunity for you to find the greatest fulfillment in providing service to others.

CHAPTER NINE

◆ ◆ ◆

YOU ARE SO MUCH MORE THAN YOU THINK YOU ARE

All is God, God is Spirit, and Spirit is All. Does this mean that there is no place where the Spirit of God leaves off and man-woman begins? In answering this question, consider that Spirit is Infinite, which means no limitations—endless, boundless. We also think of Spirit as Omnipresent, being fully present in all places at all times; Omniscient, possessing total Knowledge, all Wisdom; and Omnipotent, the Almighty, the all Power. Now consider that Spirit is Infinite, Omnipresent, Omniscient, Omnipotent *Energy*—energy being defined as the vitality of expression.

Imagine now that this All-Knowing, All-Powerful Energy, everywhere present, is pulsating to a particular Divine Vibration of Mind. Since it is the nature of this Universal Mind Energy to express Itself, can we not intuit the idea that as this Omnipresence begins to conceive of Individual Being—*You*—

the vibration of this Energy Field begins to change at the point of conception?

Think along these lines for a moment. The Universal Spirit gives "birth" to a new vibration within Itself, and the resulting Consciousness is Spirit being Self-conscious of Itself as Individualized Being—*You!* The word *individualized* means an *indivisible* entity. Therefore, the Universal Presence cannot separate Itself, or break Itself into parts, in order to become Individual Being. It simply altered Its vibration, and *You* came forth in consciousness as a particularization of God. Yet the endlessness, the boundlessness, the continuity of Spirit remains the same.

Can you understand now that the only difference between the Universal Spirit of God and the Individualized Spirit of God *you are* is but a change in vibration? It is a stepping down in frequency to where the Universe says "I AM." This I AM is God, this I AM is You, Universal *and* Individual Consciousness—God knowing Itself as God, God knowing Itself as You, and You knowing Yourself as God.

As I pointed out in the Introduction, "When we came to dwell in the material plane and took on a physical body, a part of our Divine Consciousness was lowered in vibration for the purpose of grounding and functioning on the third-dimensional plane....Our Self-awareness became the medium between Spirit and the material world, interpreting spiritual ideas as form and experience." This has been considered "the second creation"— but rather than separating Itself, which It could not do, the Divine Self simply changed the vibratory rate within the center of Its individualized energy field. In this "pressed out" state of consciousness you knew yourself to be as you were in the beginning and continued to be—the Spirit of God in expression, fully aware of your Self.

When you took on form, the creative energy of your God-Mind was stepped down in vibration for both the nonphysical and physical bodies. This did not give you a new identification as a body, for you are not such a thing. You have one, but you are not it. The physical body is simply energy-in-form—a vehicle to use on the dense physical plane—while the true Body remains invisible as pure Light. So we see now that the Universal Spirit, the Individualized Soul or Self, and the Body are all the energy of God in differing degrees of vibration—and that it is impossible for there to be any line of demarcation between God and what we call man and woman. There is no place where God leaves off and a "person" begins. All is God and God is all!

Spiritual Activity

The only "separation" between you and God is the *belief* in separation. To replace that false conviction with Truth, spend time each day with the following meditative exercise.

Before you begin, understand that there are seven energy centers in the etheric body called chakras, each representing different levels of consciousness. In the treatment, focus your attention in the area of the particular chakra, and meditate on the corresponding idea for several minutes—then move up to the next level. This exercise is not related to the esoteric work of awakening the energy centers. It is simply a method used to transmute the energies of lower mind to a higher frequency—into the Christ Vibration where there is no sense of separation.

Say to yourself: *I am much more than I think I am.*

Now focus on the appropriate chakra and think about the following:

Root chakra near the reproductive organs: *I am more than a physical body.*

Sacral chakra near the navel: *I am more than personality, more than the thoughts of my mind.*

Solar plexus chakra: *I am more than feelings and emotions.*

Heart chakra: *I am the unconditional Love of Christ in expression as me, and the fullness of Spirit dwells in me.*

Throat chakra: *I am the Christ Consciousness of Power and Dominion. I am the Creative Master of my world.*

Third eye chakra, between the brows: *I am the Christ of God in whom the Father is well pleased. I am illumined. I see only the Reality of God.*

Crown chakra, above the top of the head: *I am one with the Universe. I am the Universe. I and my Father are one. All that the Father is, I am. I am the Spirit of the Living God.*

CHAPTER TEN

◆ ◆ ◆

WORKING IN THE ENERGY
OF THE ABSOLUTE

In realizing the fulfillment of desires, you must have the consciousness for the thing desired. Without the consciousness, the thing cannot come to you; with the consciousness, it *must* come. As the eminent metaphysician Emmet Fox has written, "The secret of successful living is to build up the mental equivalent that you want; and to get rid of, to expunge, the mental equivalent that you do not want."[1] Remember that a mental equivalent is a conviction, a subconscious pattern, a realization, a subjective comprehension of Truth.

The first step in building a mental equivalent is to recognize that the Divine Idea corresponding to your desire is already within your Superconsciousness. Think of it this way: The spiritual prototype of everything visible is a part of the energy field that is around and within you. In essence, you already have—*right* now—everything that you could possibly desire, not only for this life, but for all eternity. For example, money is a spiritual idea, as is food, clothing, shelter, transportation, the right work, the perfect body, the ideal mate, and everything else that is manifest as visible form and experience. And all of these spiritual ideas are part of you—they are yours *now*, just waiting to express in mind and then in the physical world. Remember that everything is stepped down from the spiritual to the mental to the physical.

In order to build a mental equivalent, there must be a fusion of thought and feeling along the lines of a particular desire-fulfillment. To set the stage for this fusion, recall from the previous chapter that your entire being is the energy of God in differing degrees of vibration. There is no place where God leaves off and you begin. All is God in various levels of expression—and these expressions are active within you now to help you on the evolutionary spiral back to your full awakening.

I am talking about three distinct vibrations of energy. The first one is the energy of the *Absolute*, the pure life, pure love, and pure intelligence of your God-Self, the Reality of you. This is the realm of Cause.

Another vibration of energy is the *Energy of Action*. This is the phase of mind that works with the Law of Cause and Effect. It is the creative power of the lower planes, and functions as a "laboratory" where mental equivalents are formed. In modern psychology, it is called the subjective or subconscious mind.

Another is the *Energy of Awareness*, or the energy of the relative consciousness, commonly referred to as the objective mind.

When the *action energy*—or subconscious mind—receives instructions direct from the *awareness energy*—or objective mind, it will begin to form subjective patterns based on relative conditions, qualifications, and precedents. For example, let's say that you are treating for success and prosperity, and you affirm that you are now in your true place with an all-sufficiency of supply. If you affirm primarily out of a relative consciousness, you will be giving the creative power every kind of restriction that may happen to be in your consciousness at the time. In fact, you may be thinking something like this: "I am affirming great success and prosperity in my life, but I really know that there are only certain channels through which my good can come, and I believe that only a certain amount of that good can come forth at this time, and there will probably be a delay because my horoscope says that my houses of career success and finances are not in the right spots." You can see what kind of mental equivalent you will get from that kind of thinking.

When you treat or affirm out of the lower level of relative consciousness, your demonstration will always be dependent on your preconceived ideas. You will do your very best to think of ways that your good can be restricted—or you will consider only one channel through which your good can come—and your reasoning mind may tell you that there is no way the good can come today.

But when you tune into your Higher Self and take on the Christ Vibration, you are literally moving out of the relative energy and into the energy of the Absolute. And when you speak the word out of this higher consciousness, your subconscious will comprehend the Truth and will establish the patterns on the basis of *no* limitations, *no* restrictions, *no* time element, and *no* past history. It will operate strictly on the basis of Principle, the Principle of Fulfillment and Abundance that is already your True Nature. It will accept the spiritual prototype from the Absolute and duplicate that spiritual idea as a mental equivalent, rather than take your preconceived ideas and build sandcastles that will wash away.

When you speak from and as the Absolute, the pattern through which the creative energy of God-Mind radiates is perfect, and as this energy flows through the perfect pattern, it takes on all the attributes of the Ideal and goes forth into the outer world to manifest corresponding circumstances, experiences, and form. Spiritual ideas from the realm of Cause are what we are seeking when we pray, "Thy kingdom come, Thy will be done, in earth as it is in heaven." And this is also the meaning of Psalm 127: "Except the Lord build the house, they labor in vain that build it."

Spiritual Activity

Prior to the use of your affirmations today, take time to quiet the mind, let go of the appearances of the outer world, and meditate on the Wholeness and Completeness of your Divine Self. Use this idea as you take the inner journey:

Closer than breathing is the Presence of God I AM...absolute harmony, perfect love, infinite wisdom... the only power, the only cause, the only activity of my eternal life.

Contemplate the meaning behind the words, and let the spiritual vibration fill your consciousness—then listen as the Voice within speaks to you of your divinity, your holiness. Continuing in this high state of consciousness, speak the word for your good, affirming total fulfillment as the Holy Self you are, and calling forth into visibility that which you already have.

CHAPTER ELEVEN

REACHING MOUNTAINTOP CONSCIOUSNESS

What is the most effective way to scale the mountain? Jesus gave us the answer when he talked about the Commandment that is the first and greatest of all. He said, "Thou shalt love the Lord thy God with all thy heart, and with all thy soul, and with all thy mind, and with all thy strength." Now the Lord *your* God is the Spirit of God within you—and you are told to love this Presence with your entire being, with everything you've got. Do you know what it means to love something totally? It means to have constant and continuous adoration for that something, to be so filled with devotion, affection, tenderness, warmth, admiration, rapture, and love toward that something that your entire consciousness is taken over by it.

Understand this: When you contemplate that Presence within—your very Spirit—with great love, that one-pointed love-focus will literally draw the awesome and incredible Power of the universe right into your thinking mind and feeling nature. You take on the Power and you become the Power and you speak as the Power—and behold—all things are made new. Your thoughts of abundance produce abundance, your feelings of wholeness produce wellness in your body, your vision of success is manifest, your words of love bring forth the relationship you've been seeking.

When the spiritual masters of the past told us to love the true nature of our being, our Spiritual Reality, only a few people on this planet understood that this was a secret formula for health, wealth, and happiness. Only a handful interpreted it from the standpoint of practical everyday living. Only a small percentage recognized it to be the combination to the Storehouse. To love your God-Self is the greatest Commandment because within it are the secrets of the universe. And you can track this master teaching all the way back to the beginning of the Mystery Schools. It was taught by all the seers, sages, saints, and master souls of the distant past—and one of the most comprehensive teachings is found in Deuteronomy.

In Deuteronomy 6:5-9 we are told:

> *And thou shalt love the Lord thy God with all thine heart, and with all thy soul, and with all thy might. And these words, which I command thee this day, shall be in thine heart: And thou shalt teach them diligently unto thy children, and shalt talk of them when thou sittest in thine house, and when thou walkest by the way, and when thou liest down, and when thou risest up. And they shalt be as frontlets between thine eyes. And thou shalt write them upon the posts of thy house, and on thy gates.*

Talk about dedicating your life to the love of Christ within! And when you do, your world will change dramatically. You see, when you direct your attention within and focus that feeling of intense love toward your Higher Self, the entire vibration of your energy field is lifted up to be in tune with the Divine Vibration. And when this happens, you become a transparency for the Activity of God. The radiating Power from within will then dissolve old error patterns, false beliefs, and negative appearances, and will move through you to appear as every needed thing in your life. And the Spirit within is so practical! If you need a better job, one will be attracted to you. If you need more money, it will come in streams of abundance. If you need a healing, the wholeness will be manifest in your body. If you need a new relationship, the right "meeting" will be arranged. You will be shown that there is the perfect supply for every demand.

Spiritual Activity

Let's take the instructions from Deuteronomy and put them into a nine-step program for daily living:

Step No. 1: We are told that these words (loving the Spirit of God within) "shall be in thine heart." This means to impress your subconscious mind with your love of God through daily meditations—by contemplating your inner Being with all the love, adoration, and emotion you can feel. Spend time each day in "tender passion" with your God-Self.

Step No. 2: We are told that "thou shalt teach (the love of our God-Self) diligently unto thy children." Your children are your thoughts, so you begin now to train your mind—teaching it to relate only to the One Presence and Power within—and to love your Christ Self joyfully and gratefully. Whenever a negative thought enters your mind during the day, gently but firmly say, "I choose to control my thoughts by laying aside every weight and turning within to the One I love with all my heart, mind, and soul." Then think on that Inner Presence with great love.

Step No. 3: We are told to talk of this love of our Christ Self "when thou sittest in thine house." The house is your consciousness, and to "sit" in consciousness refers to prayer or spiritual treatment. Therefore, you begin your spiritual activity by first focusing your love on the Christ within and drawing that reciprocal Love Power into your consciousness.

Step No. 4: We are told to love our Higher Self "when thou walkest by the way." This means that even in moments of idle thinking—when you are simply contemplating the activities of "this world"—you are not to forget the courtship of your True Self. The dominant trend of your thoughts must now be in this direction, regardless of what you are doing.

Step No. 5: We are told to focus that love "when thou liest down." In other words, before you go to sleep at night, again express your deep feelings of love for your beautiful Christ Self. Just say, "I love you so very much. You are so fine, so wonderful, and my love for you fills my entire being to overflowing."

Step No. 6: We are told to express that love "when thou risest up." Train yourself to begin each new day by acknowledging your Higher Self and pouring out all the love you can feel in your heart toward that Master Consciousness within. Say: "Through my love for you, I dedicate this day to you. I seek only your will, your word, your way, your work. I let my light so shine this day that I only glorify you."

Step No. 7: We are told that we shall bind this love of our Higher Self "for a sign upon thine hand." Now the hand stands for the expressing of God's ideas in the material world—and we are the channels for that expression in our daily activities. Therefore, we are told to bind—or insure—that we make our daily work a symbol or a sign of our love of God. So do everything that is in front of you to the best of your ability, if for no other reason than for the love of your God-Self.

Step No. 8: We are told that this love for our Inner Self "be as frontlets between thine eyes." That is a direct reference to the creative imagination faculty within all of us, so words and feelings of love for your Christ Self will lift up your vision, expand your consciousness, and enable you to see with new clarity and spiritual understanding.

Step No. 9: And finally, we are told that we shall write these words of love for our Higher Self "upon the posts of thy house, and on thy gates." In other words, keep the love your God-Self right in the forefront of your consciousness—right within your thinking-objective mind—moment by moment, hour by hour, day by day.

If you will make these nine steps an integral part of your daily living, your life will be forever changed. You will be a new creature—"alive with God and upheld by His free Spirit forever."

Chapter Twelve

$\diamond$ ◆ $\diamond$

Health and Healing

All of creation—the infinite universes and all that is visible and invisible—is energy in motion. It is the Thinkingness and Knowingness of God-Mind—Divine Ideas in a state of continuous manifestation. The Spirit of God is pure Cosmic Energy, and this spiritual substance is individualized as each man, each woman. Therefore, each one of us is an energy field pulsating to a divine vibration. This is our Life Force—the pure Energy of God—and as this Energy lowers its rate of vibration, physical form takes place, manifesting as cells, tissue, and organs according to the Perfect Body Idea (the Word). And the Word is made flesh.

Ideas such as sickness, disease, and old age do not exist in the Mind of God. Therefore, as the pure Energy of God-Mind expresses as the Life Principle and forms the body according to the Perfect Pattern, the visible manifestation must also be perfect. Since we were created out of perfection, we must be perfect. But how do we explain the appearance of disease and sickness? Go back to the principle that in the Mind of God, thoughts are creative, and since we are individualizations of God, our thoughts are also creative. We have the freedom to create conditions and experiences in our lives according to the thoughts we think and accept as true. Thus, we create our own diseases by objectifying fear, hate, worry, or other mental-emotional disturbances. But we can also be restored to our normal state of perfection through the right use of our minds.

Any idea that is registered as a conviction in our deeper mind results in a change in our world, beginning with the body. When we begin to consider that the healing principle within is the Cause of our physical well-being, the negative energy within our individual force field begins to change. In other words, physical perfection is the natural state of our being, and as this Truth is accepted in our thinking and feeling natures, our bodies will change accordingly. So a "healing" is simply a return to our natural state.

Based on my research into the subject of health and healing, I believe that an individual can return to his/her natural state of perfection by working with the four "bodies" that comprise individual being: the spiritual, emotional, mental, and physical bodies. In the spiritual realm, we dedicate ourselves to realizing our True Nature by working from the vantage point that we are spiritual beings—to awaken to the truth of our Divine Identity. This is the purpose of meditation, where we dwell upon our inner Reality, knowing that whatever we contemplate is drawn into our consciousness. This focus on the Christ within will also begin to awaken the subconscious to "remember" the true Image of Self—the Divine Perfection that we are. So meditation is the foundation for both a restoration and a preventive "medicine" program. Through meditation, you will be raising the vibration of your energy field to the divine frequency, thus opening the way for the healing currents to move through every atom of your being.

In working with the emotional body, do whatever is necessary to immediately rid yourself of all negative feelings such as unforgiveness, resentment, criticism, fear, and jealousy. Even the American Medical Association is talking about the cause-and-effect relationship between emotions and wellness. In the January 14, 1983 issue of *The Journal of the American Medical Association,* it was reported that "...investigators found that gum-disease patients had experienced more negative, unsettling life events in the previous year than other people...they also demonstrated higher levels of anxiety, depression, and emotional disturbances."

We have found that the use of spiritual treatments can reverse deep-seated emotional patterns and clear a path for the Inner Power to act. For example, if there is unforgiveness in your heart toward anyone (a parent thought for arthritis, cancer, and heart problems), sit quietly and state firmly and lovingly: "I forgive you totally and completely. I hold no unforgiveness in my heart toward anyone, and if there is anything in my consciousness that even resembles unforgiveness, I cast it upon the indwelling Christ to be dissolved right now. I forgive everyone and I am free!"

Work with such statements, adapting and changing the words for any negative emotion, until you feel a sense of release and there is no longer a negative attachment to the person or experience. You can also use the 10-step manifestation process (in my book *Empowerment*[1]) to eliminate negative feelings and emotions. Choose a master thought—a Divine Idea—to replace the negative pattern. Accept it with all your heart, and embody it with a sense of *have*. Then see yourself free of the emotional attachment, and express a deep feeling of love. Speak the word that it is done, and surrender your entire being to the Spirit within with great thankfulness. Then move out into your world as a fearless, flawless, and free Child of the Living God.

When we come down to managing our thought processes, we are actually working with the mental body. As Louise L. Hay says in her book *Heal Your Body:*

> Stop for a moment and catch your thought. What are you thinking right now? If thoughts shape your life and experiences, would you want this thought to become true for you? If it is a thought of worry or anger or hurt or revenge, how do you think this thought will come back to you? If we want a joyous life, we must think joyous thoughts. If we want a prosperous life, we must think prosperous thoughts. If we want a loving life, we must think loving thoughts. Whatever we send out mentally or verbally will come back to us in like form. Listen to the words you say. If you hear yourself saying something three times, write it down. It has become a pattern for you. At the end of a week, look at the list you have made and you will see how your words fit your experience. Be willing to change your words and thoughts, and watch your life change. It's your power and your choice. No one thinks in your mind but you.[2]

Remember that the use of creative imagination and visualization techniques also relates to your mental body and greatly influences the physical system. See yourself well! Visualize your wholeness, the natural state of your being. Cancer patients, for example, are benefiting from what is called "positive-image therapy." It combines relaxation techniques with teaching the patient to imagine the body's natural cancer-fighting forces—the white blood cells, for instance—and to visualize that the cancer is vulnerable to the treatment. In a study at the Washington School of Psychiatry, six patients led by Dr. Robert Kvarnes had blood samples analyzed before and after the training. The result was that the number of white cells and the amount of a chemical called thymosin in their blood increased. Both changes indicated that the patients' immune systems were stronger.

Regarding the physical body, I believe that we must always work from the standpoint of where we are in consciousness and not "gamble" by taking action that is beyond our belief system. What I am saying is this: God works through both the metaphysician and the physician. However, healing cannot be complete until the negative patterns in consciousness are corrected. Therefore, medical assistance may offer only temporary relief. Also, a doctor may not be necessary if the individual will combine spiritual work with a good physical health program—that is, the proper diet, exercise, and good judgment in the maintenance of the body. Nutrition experts can give you valuable information on vitamins and minerals, and excellent books on physical fitness can be found in every bookstore. Rather than advise you personally on these particular "outer" activities, I suggest that you: (1) Go within for specific guidance regarding your own situation and what is needed in the manifest world to maintain your body in top physical condition, and (2) Follow that guidance and establish your special health program of foods, supplements, exercise, body cleansing, natural substitutes for drugs, and so on. We each have to find what is right for us—individually.

Spiritual Activity

Let's base our spiritual work on bringing the spiritual, emotional, mental, and physical bodies into perfect alignment.

Earlier I discussed the effects of meditation as a "foundation for both a restoration and preventive 'medicine' program." The form of meditation I am recommending here to realize the true nature of Wholeness is called a "meditative treatment." If you are experiencing a health problem, it means there is a false belief in your consciousness that is outpicturing itself as a malady in your body. There is a misconception and a misunderstanding in your mind regarding the natural state of your being. To meet this challenge, you must replace the error with Truth in consciousness, and this can be done most effectively through this type of meditation.

This is the statement that we will work with in the meditative treatment:

The Spirit of God is the Life Force within me, and every cell of my body is filled with the intelligence, love, and radiant energy of God-Mind.

God's will for me is perfect health, and God sees me as perfect; therefore wellness is the natural state of my being.

Ideas such as sickness, disease, and old age cannot exist in the Mind of God. That Mind is my mind, so I now see myself as God sees me...strong, vital, perfect.

I am now lifted up into the Consciousness of Wholeness. I accept my healing. I am healed now! And it is so.

Now become very still and relaxed, then slowly and with feeling, read the statement again, meditating on each word, contemplating each sentence until the true meaning registers in your consciousness. Remember that words are only symbols; it is the idea behind the word that has power. So meditate on the idea until there is an inner understanding and realization. I will lead you through the first meditation, but in subsequent treatments, let your own thoughts replace my words.

Meditation

The Spirit of God (Contemplate the idea—the meaning behind the words—of the Spirit of God until you feel something within. Speak the words silently and watch the other thoughts that flow in to expand your thinking.)

...is the Life Force within me (Dwell on the meaning and the activity of the Life Force of God operating in and through your body. Feel the dynamics of this incredible power. Sense the renewing, restoring action of Spirit as it eliminates everything unlike itself in your body.)

...and every cell of my body is filled with the intelligence, love, and radiant energy of God-Mind. ("See" each cell pulsating with Light and Life—filled with God-Intelligence, God-Love, and God-Energy. Each cell is now thinking the thoughts of God, expressing the Love of God and vibrating in harmony with the peace of God. Contemplate this.)

...God's will for me is perfect health (Think of God's will as the cosmic urge to express perfection, which is being done in your body at this moment.)

...and God sees me as perfect (This is the Vision of God projecting the Reality of Perfection throughout every cell, organ, and tissue of your body. Ponder this.)

...therefore, wellness is the natural state of my being. (What God sees is the Reality behind the illusion. This Divine Vision, this Holy Seeingness, is permeating your entire being. Feel this.)

...Ideas such as sickness, disease, and old age cannot exist in the Mind of God. (If such ideas do not exist, they cannot be manifest, therefore it is your ideas that have been expressed as a negative physical condition. You are

now aware of this, and you know that you have the divine authority to replace those error thoughts with Truth ideas, and you now make the definite decision to do so.)

...*That Mind is my mind* (There is but one Mind— God-Mind. That Mind is in expression as your mind. Your mind, being a part of God-Mind, has the Holy Power of Spirit. And you are now using that Power in cooperating with God. Contemplate God's Mind expressing as your mind, and your mind expressing God's Ideas of Perfection.)

...*so I now see as God sees me...strong, vital, vibrant, perfect.* (Lift up your vision and see as God sees. See Wholeness. See Wellness. See Divine Order. See Perfection. See God *as* your body.)

...*I am now lifted up into the Consciousness of Wholeness.* (Feel the pure vibration of Love, Life, and Light as you rise into the very Presence of Spirit. Meditate on the spiritual energy that now surrounds you, engulfs you, and flows in and through you. Let go and give yourself to the magnificent healing currents.

...*I accept my healing. I am healed now! And it is so.* (When you accept your healing, you have taken the final step. Where there was darkness, there is now Light. Where there was error, there is now Truth. Where there was imperfection, there is now Perfection. You are healed! Acknowledge now that it is so.)

Remain in the consciousness of Spirit for a few more minutes, in communion with your God-Self. In this spiritual vibration you will be highly successful in dealing with your emotional body. Forgiving others will be easy, and old hurts, resentments, and other negative feelings can quickly be cast upon the Christ within to be dissolved. For this particular activity, make a list of everyone who could possibly need your forgiveness, then speak their name aloud and say: "I forgive you. I choose to do this now, and I hold nothing back. I forgive you totally and completely."

Next, take an imaginary box and in your mind, fill it with every hurt, resentment, condemnation, depressed feeling, anger thought, and any other negative patterns you find in consciousness. Take the box and see yourself lovingly placing it upon the Holy Fire of Spirit Within where it is totally consumed.

To properly manage your thought process, refer back to the words on page 82 from Louise Hay's book *Heal Your Body*, and begin to listen to the words you say throughout the day. What habit patterns are you forming? Start exercising control over the thoughts you think and the words you speak. Practice thinking joyful, loving, prosperous, and harmonious thoughts. Train yourself to think and speak only according to the Christ standard, and use your power of creative imagination to see yourself as whole, well, and perfect.

In working with the physical body, ask yourself: "What do I intuitively feel I must do in the manifest world to maintain my body in top physical condition?" Whatever the answer, be sure to follow your inner guidance in establishing a health program that is right for your individual consciousness.

Work daily to keep your four bodies in holy agreement, and sickness will be a thing of the past for you.

Chapter Thirteen

$$\diamond \quad \diamond \quad \diamond$$

The Principle of Abundance

As you gain the understanding of the Principle of Abundance and realize the Truth therein, you will be free of all lack, limitation, and imperfection—beginning with your body and continuing out to encompass all conditions, situations, circumstances, and experiences of your life and affairs. Reason: Your outer world will be a reflection, an outpicturing, of Truth rather than the false beliefs of the ego.

Do you have an aversion to wealth? Do you object to being rich? Does the word *abundance* bother you? If you say yes, you do not believe in God—because God is omnipresent Wealth, the infinite Riches of the universe, the lavish Abundance of creation. And if you deny unlimited prosperity, you are denying yourself, because *you* are the image of omnipresent wealth, the expression of the infinite riches of the universe, an individualization of lavish abundance. You are as rich right now as any individual who ever walked on this planet. The cattle on a thousand hills are yours, the gold and silver are yours, and an abundance of money is yours now!

If you enjoy reading the Bible, you'll find that God indeed loves prosperity:

> *Beloved, I wish above all things that thou mayest prosper.*
>
> *Prove me now herewith, said the Lord of hosts, if I will not open you the windows of heaven and pour you out a blessing, that there shall not be room enough to receive it.*
>
> *The blessing of the Lord, it maketh rich, and He addeth no sorrow with it.*
>
> *They shall prosper that love Thee. Peace be within thy walls, and prosperity within thy palaces.*
>
> *God is able to make all grace abound toward you; that ye, always having all-sufficiency in all things may abound to every good work.*
>
> *Thou shalt remember the Lord thy God, for it is He that giveth thee power to get wealth.*
>
> *The Lord shall open unto thee His good treasure, the heaven to give the rain unto thy land in His season, and to bless all the work of thine hand; and thou shalt lend unto many nations, and thou shalt not borrow.*
>
> *Let the Lord be magnified which hath pleasure in the prosperity of His servant.*

Your Lord is the Spirit of God, the Christ within. You magnify this Master Self that you are in truth by realizing that you and God are one. All that this one Presence and Power is, you are—and all that this Infinite Mind has, is yours. Above you, around you, in and through you, is *You*, the Reality of You, an omnipotent Force Field embodying all Love, all Wisdom, all Life, all Substance, all ALL. This Allness that is individualized as you is the same Mind, the same Spirit, who spoke to Moses from the burning bush, the One who spoke through Jesus.

This Spirit within you is forever thinking thoughts of Abundance, which is its true nature. Since thoughts of lack or limitation can never be registered or entertained in this Infinite Mind, then the Principle of Law of Supply must be one of total and continuous All-Sufficiency. Your Self thinks, sees, and knows only abundance, and the creative energy of this Mind-of-Abundance is eternally flowing, radiating, expressing, seeking to appear as abundance on the physical plane.

This radiating creative Mind Energy is substance. As this Divine Thought Energy flows through your consciousness and out into the phenomenal world to appear as prosperous experiences and conditions, its "plastic" quality allows it to be impressed by the tone and shape of your dominant beliefs. Therefore, what you see, hear, taste, touch, and smell are your beliefs objectified. The form and the experience are but effects—appearances—and we are told to not judge by appearances. To "judge" something means to believe it, to assume that it is true, to conclude that it is factual. But we are advised not to do this. Why? Because what appears as an effect has no value in itself. The only attributes that an effect has are the ones that you give it.

Money is an effect. When you concentrate on the effect, you are forgetting the cause, and when you forget the cause, the effect begins to diminish. When you focus your attention on getting money, you are actually shutting off your supply. You must begin this very moment to cease believing that money is your substance, your supply, your support, your security, or your safety. Money is not—but God is. When you understand and realize this Truth, the supply flows uninterrupted into perfect and abundant manifestation. You must look to God alone as the Source, and take your mind completely off the outer effect.

If you look to your job, your employer, your spouse, or your investments as the source of your supply, you are cutting off the real Source. In fact, if you look to any human person, place, or condition for your supply, you are shutting down the flow. If you give power to any mortal as even being the channel for your supply, you are limiting your good.

You must think of money and any other material desire or possession simply as an outer symbol of the inner supply. And the only Reality of that symbol is the substance that underlies the outward manifestation. Money is the symbol of an Idea in Divine Mind (as is every other good thing). The Idea is an all-sufficiency of supply to meet every need with a divine surplus in your life. As the Divine Idea comes out into manifestation, it appears as the symbol: money. But the money is not the supply. Rather, it is your consciousness of God *as* your abundance that constitutes your supply. When you try to collect, acquire, and possess the symbol (focusing on the symbol and not the supply within), the outlet for the manifestation closes.

Do you want more money, more prosperity in your life? Then shift from a consciousness of effects (materiality) to a consciousness of cause (spirituality). When you give power to an effect, you are giving it *your* power. You are actually giving the effect power over you. Does money have power? If you say yes, you have given it your power and you have become the servant. You have reversed the roles.

The Inner Presence—the You of you—is truly the money-maker. Your thinking, reasoning mind is not. Your only Source is the God Presence within you. If your mind is on the effect, you block the flow. The more impersonal you become regarding where your money seems to originate (job, salary, commissions, investments, spouse, and so on), the more personal you can become in your relationship with the true Source of your money, and the closer the relationship to your God-Self, the greater the abundance in your life.

Turn within and watch the Inner Presence work. The activity of your Infinite Mind sees and knows only abundance—and in this sea of Knowingness is a spiritual Idea corresponding to every single form, event, circumstance, condition, or experience that you could possibly desire. The creative energy of these Divine Ideas is forever flowing into perfect manifestation. But remember, if you constantly look to the effect, the visible form, you will create a mutation, a less-than-perfect manifestation. By keeping your focus on Spirit, however, you will keep the channel open for the externalization of Spirit according to the Divine Idea.

The time must come when you will satisfy a need for money by steadfastly depending on the Master Self within and not on anything in the outer world of form. Until you do this, you will continue to experience the uncertainties of supply. You must learn this lesson, and until you do, you will be given opportunity after opportunity in the form of apparent lack and limitation. You may be experiencing such a challenge right at this moment. Realize that this is the opportunity you have been waiting for to demonstrate the Truth of your birthright. Know that this entire experience is but an illusion, an outpicturing of your beliefs, an effect of your consciousness. But you are going to stop giving any power to the illusion, the effect. You are going to cease feeding it with negative energy. You are going to withdraw your energy from the outer scene and let it die, let it fade back into the nothingness from which it came.

Take your stand this day as a spiritual being, and renounce all claims to humanhood and mortality. Care not what is going on in your world, regardless of your fears about your creditors, your security, your protection, your future. Turn away from the effects, wave good-bye to external false belief pictures, and return to the Father's House where you have belonged ever since you left under the spell of materiality. Take your mind off money and material possessions, and focus only on the lavish abundance of divine substance that is forever flowing from that Master Consciousness within you. Take your stand and prove God now!

Stop adding up your bills stop counting the money you have or need, and stop looking for your supply from any mortal person, place, or situation. The whole Universe is standing on tip-toe watching you—praying that you will let go of the negative appearances of the world of illusion and claim your divine heritage. Now is the time, today is the day. Pass this test and you will never have to go through it again. But if you yield to mortal pressure and carnal mind temptation to get temporary financial relief from the world of effects, you will have to go back to the classroom and learn the lesson all over again.

Say to yourself with great feeling:

This day (speak the actual date) I cease believing in visible money as my supply and my support, and I view the world of effect as it truly is—simply an outpicturing of my former beliefs. I believed in the power of money; therefore, I surrendered my God-given power and authority to an objectified belief. I believed in the possibility of lack, thus causing a separation in consciousness from the Source of my supply. I believed in mortal man and carnal conditions, and through this faith, gave man and conditions power over me. I believed in the mortal illusion created by the collective consciousness of error thoughts, and in doing so I have limited the Unlimited. No more! This day I renounce my so-called humanhood and claim my divine inheritance as a Being of God. This day I acknowledge God and only God as my substance, my supply, and my support.

Now impress these statements of Principle on your mind:

1. *God is lavish, unfailing Abundance, the rich omnipresent substance of the Universe. This all- providing Source of infinite prosperity is individualized as me, as the Reality of me.*

2. *I lift up my mind and heart to be aware, to understand, and to know that the Divine Presence I AM is the Source and Substance of all my good.*

3. *I am conscious of the Inner Presence as my lavish Abundance. I am conscious of the constant activity of this Mind of infinite Prosperity. Therefore, my consciousness is filled with the Light of Truth.*

4. *Through my consciousness of my God-Self, the Christ within, as my Source, I draw into my mind and feeling nature the very substance of Spirit. This substance is my supply; thus, my consciousness of the Presence of God within me is my supply.*

5. *Money is not my supply. No person, place, or condition is my supply. My awareness, understanding, and knowledge of the all-providing activity of Divine Mind within me is my supply. My consciousness of this Truth is unlimited; therefore, my supply is unlimited.*

6. *My inner supply instantly and constantly takes on form and experience according to my needs and desires, and as the Principle of Supply in action, it is impossible for me to have any needs or unfulfilled desires.*

7. *The Divine Consciousness that I am is forever expressing its true nature of Abundance. This is its responsibility—not mine. My only responsibility is to be aware of this Truth. Therefore, I am totally confident in letting go and letting God appear as the abundant all-sufficiency in my life and affairs.*

8. *My consciousness of the Spirit within me as my unlimited Source is the Divine Power to restore the years the locusts have eaten, to make all things new, to lift me up to the High Road of abundant prosperity. This awareness, understanding, and knowledge of Spirit appears as every visible form and experience I could possibly desire.*

9. *When I am aware of the God-Self within me as my total fulfillment, I am totally fulfilled. I am now aware of this Truth. I have found the secret of life, and I relax in the knowledge that the Activity of Divine Abundance is eternally operating in my life. I simply have to be aware of the flow, the radiation, of that Creative Energy, which is continuously, easily, and effortlessly pouring from my Divine Consciousness. I am now aware. I am now in the flow.*

10. *I keep my mind and thoughts off "this world," and I place my entire focus on God within as the only Cause of my prosperity. I acknowledge the Inner Presence as the only activity in my financial affairs, as the substance of all things visible. I place my faith in the Principle of Abundance in action within me.*

Spiritual Activity

Here is a program for realizing abundant prosperity in your life and affairs. It takes 40 days for consciousness to realize, or develop a subjective comprehension of, a truth. A break during the 40-day period releases the energy being built up around the idea. Therefore, there must be a definite commitment to faithfully follow this program each and every day for 40 days—and if you miss even one day, to start over again and continue until you can go the full period with perfect continuity. Here is the course of action:

1. Establish a specific date to start your program, such as the beginning of a particular week. Count out 40 days on your calendar, and mark the completion date.

2. On the first day of the program, write in your workbook the entire statement shown earlier that begins with "This day I cease believing in visible money as my supply and my support..."

3. There are 10 statements of Principle. Read *one* statement each day. This means that you will go through the entire list *four times* during the 40-day period.

4. After reading the daily statement—either upon aris-
ing or before going to bed in the evening—meditate
on it for at least 15 minutes, focusing on each idea in
the statement with great thoughtfulness and feeling,
letting the ideas fill your consciousness.

5. Following each meditation period, write in your
workbook the thoughts that come to you. Be sure to
do this daily.

6. If you are working in a Master Mind or study group,
exchange the thoughts written in your workbooks
and discuss them in the group for greater illumination and understanding.

7. Since you have *already* received an all-sufficiency of
supply (all that Infinite Mind has is yours now), you
can prove this Truth to your deeper mind by sharing
your supply on a regular basis. Giving is an esoteric
science that never fails to produce results if it is done
with love and joy, because the Law will shower you
with a pressed down and multiplied return. But if
you tithe (and I really prefer the word *sharing* to
tithing) as a mechanical and calculated method to
please God, unload guilt, meet a sense of obligation,
and play a bartering game with the Law, no one benefits—not even the receiver. Give with love, joy, and
a sense of fun, and the windows of heaven will be
thrown open with a blast.

Chapter Fourteen

❖ ❖ ❖

Your Consciousness Is Your Faith

The entire Universe is nothing but pure God Energy—vibrating, thinking, knowing—omnipresent, omniscient, omnipotent. And within this Divine Radiance is the attribute of Absolute Faith—total belief, total confidence, total trust, total certainty, and total conviction in Itself.

As this Infinite Presence and Power of Absolute Fidelity expresses *as* you, as It brings the whole thrust of the Universe into individualization, It also brings with It the incredible Energy of Faith to serve as one of your Divine Powers. This Power is the very foundation of your Soul, the energy of your consciousness.

Faith *is* your consciousness. You think, feel, speak, and act according to your consciousness, according to your faith. Faith is the substance (the creative energy) of things hoped for, the evidence of things unseen; therefore, your consciousness is that which stands under and supports (the substance of) that which you are experiencing in your world. Your consciousness is the *present* evidence of what you will experience in your life as your thoughts and emotions are externalized.

If your consciousness is filled with fear and anxiety, that is where your faith is. You are putting your faith in the possibility and probability of misfortune, lack, and limitation. Your consciousness, which is your faith, your substance, must by law act upon itself. Thus, you, as Creative Energy, will create in your world exactly those conditions you fear (have faith in).

Everything in your life is vibrating according to a certain pitch and frequency. Your body, home, car, clothes, job, relationships, and money are all energy in motion—all vibrating in absolute exactness to the vibration of your consciousness. Your faith vibration attracts that which you have and experience in this world because *like must attract like!* Where is your faith? Look around you. If your faith is an all-sufficiency, then so it is in your life. If your faith is pulsating to a "just getting by" frequency, then so it is in your world. If your faith is on the dial-set of insufficiency, then there will never be enough to meet your needs. Your world simply reflects your faith.

The faculty of *Divine* faith (faith energy pulsating according to its divine vibration) may represent only a tiny particle of light within your lower mind at the present time. But Jesus said that if your faith was no larger than a grain of mustard seed (or just a faint glow of light), you could level a mountain. Now Jesus didn't kid around. When he made a statement, you could bet your life on it. But then we ask: "What about that mountain of debt, this peak of despair in my relationships, that volcano that has erupted in my body, those rising fears regarding my career?" Could the answer be that you have not recognized this Power Center as being an integral part of your individualized cosmic system?

Could it simply be that you are not *aware* that you have this inexhaustible Power right at your disposal?

Perhaps you have not been aware of the Energy of Faith, yet you have been using it. You may not have known that you had this Power, but all the time it's been the basic ingredient in all your creative activities—and many of those creations have been of a negative nature. You have created illness through the energy of faith—faith in drafts, weather, heredity, germs, viruses, old age, decay, and disease. And through your power of faith, you have created lack and limitation—faith in the economy, in money as your supply, in the intentions of others, in your own scheming and manipulating. You are not alone. We have all created a world of illusion with our faith. Every time we say that we are afraid of something, we are putting our faith in that something. What we fear most comes upon us because our faith brings it to us. If we believe that anything negative can happen in our lives, then we are vulnerable to it. If we believe in the possibility of accidents, disease, failure, or suffering of any kind, we are lowering the rate of our faith vibration and sending out negative energy to attract misfortune into our lives.

When we become aware of our Power of Faith, the energy from that Center begins to work for us according to the Divine Standard, the original High Vibration. Think of it this way: If you *do not know* that you have a certain attribute or a specific power, then your activities and decisions are based on a power outside of you. Through this belief in an outside power, you are actually transferring (giving up) a God-given power that you didn't even know you had—and you are giving it to the so-called outside forces. These forces then become the master, and you become the servant. However, when you begin to recognize that you have an incredible Power Center within your consciousness—one that represents the very Power of God—then you are calling forth the pure form of that energy to be used in transforming your life.

Spiritual Activity

Let's do something about that faith energy that you have been using in negative ways. Say to yourself, aloud and then silently with great feeling: *"I am the Power of Faith!"* Let that idea roll around in your mind for a few minutes and seep down into your emotional nature. Feel its vibration as your entire energy field begins to strengthen, firm up, and become substantial (filled with substance).

Now slowly contemplate these statements:

I believe there is NOTHING God cannot do. I believe there is nothing God cannot do THROUGH me. I believe there is nothing God cannot do AS me. God is my Self, therefore there is nothing that I cannot do. Nothing is too good for God, and nothing is too good for me!

The pure energy of Faith is now flooding your consciousness, transmuting the negative frequencies and restoring your consciousness to the spiritual vibration. And with this kind of mind-heart set, you can subdue kingdoms, bring forth righteousness, stop the mouths of lions, quench the violence of fire, and escape the edge of the sword. (See Heb. II, 11:33-34.)

The Faith Power is located in the upper part of your energy field corresponding to the center of your physical brain. Accordingly, you use your thinking mind to first contact this Power. See it with your inner vision as being halfway between your eyes and the back of your head, as a small circle of light. As you bring the light into your awareness and begin to focus on it, notice what happens. It begins to intensify, first radiating upward to fill the head, and continuing to move up until the entire upper part of your energy field is bathed in brilliant light. Then the light begins to project outward to each side of your energy field, reaching to the outer limits. Now it moves downward until it fills your entire field of consciousness with pulsating energy. Practice this exercise, knowing that as the light radiates from its center position, you are watching pure God Energy move through your mental, emotional, and physical systems—purifying, transmuting, and saturating your being with the High Vibration of Faith.

Following this exercise, bring your point of contact with the Faith Energy to your heart center by feeling the very core of this Power right in your heart. Feel the vibration, and speak these words aloud and then silently:

I love the Faith I AM with all my heart, and I now draw forth the omnipotence of this incredible energy and command it to fill my feeling nature with its Power. Come forth, my Faith! Saturate my emotions with total trust, total certainty, total conviction in myself as a being of God. I AM Substance. I AM Creative Energy. I AM God being me now. Through the pure Energy of Faith, I feel the Truth!

Now bring your point of contact with the Faith Energy up to your throat center, and feel that new strength in your throat. Speak these words aloud and then silently with great feeling:

Through the Power of Faith, I speak the word and it shall not return unto me void. I AM omnipotence made manifest on earth. I AM unlimited. I have the Power, and

I use the Power rightly and wisely and lovingly in the name of Almighty God.

Let your point of contact with the Faith Energy now be between your brows, and speak these words aloud and then silently with great concentration:

I AM a master mind, created in the image of God, and I dedicate my mind to the service of God and to all God-Kind everywhere. My mind is power-full, filled-full with the Energy of Faith, and there is nothing I cannot do.

Move your vision up to just above the top of your head, and speak these words aloud and then silently with great reverence:

I place my Faith in the Reality I AM, the very Christ of God. I now let my world reflect the Divine Activity of love, life, and abundance, for my Faith has made me whole.

Work with the Power of Faith daily, knowing that this awesome force will penetrate into the depths of consciousness and burn away all error thoughts and negative beliefs. It is the rock upon which you shall build the foundation for a full, glorious, and lasting spiritual consciousness. It is indeed the key to mastery.

CHAPTER FIFTEEN

$\blacklozenge \quad \Large\blacklozenge \quad \blacklozenge$

SPIRITUAL STRENGTH
AND WISDOM

A s the Power Center of Faith opens (awakens), its energy begins to radiate and interact with three other Centers with which it has close affinity—Strength, Wisdom, and Love. We will discuss Strength and Wisdom now, and follow with Love in the next chapter.

The Strength we are referring to here is defined as spiritual firmness and mental toughness—soundness, boldness, and steadfastness in consciousness. It means a solidifying of your awareness, understanding, and knowledge of God by eliminating all sense of spiritual weakness and revealing the majesty and magnificence of your True Nature. As the Center of Strength (positioned in your energy field near the physical location of the lower back) is awakened, it generates a feeling of poise, confidence, and great stability.

Strength is a "brother" of Faith, and if either one of these

Power Centers is lowered in vibration, the other increases its tempo to offset the loss and bring the combined energies back into balance. But this action does not take place unless you are dedicated in your efforts to awaken to your Divine Identity. The development of a spiritual consciousness and the awakening of the Power Centers go hand in hand. You cannot have one without the other.

When you begin to work with your Faith faculty, it automatically interacts with Strength, and you immediately feel that new power vibration in consciousness. Faith and Strength are now in support of one another, and if a negative condition comes to your attention and your faith drops momentarily, the power of Strength will rise up and say, "What is that to you? Do not place your faith in appearances!" And your ego counters by saying, "But there's not enough money to pay the bills." And your firm position in Spirit replies: "What do *you* know? I am strong in the Lord I AM, and I will not tolerate such an illusion. I am the Abundance of the Universe individualized, and I choose now to express an all-sufficiency to meet every need with plenty to spare and share."

Later the ego says, "I don't feel well...I think I'm going to be sick." And your mental toughness replies, "That's a lie! The Spirit of the Living God I AM is my life, and it is impossible for God's Life to be less than perfect. Therefore, I am whole, complete, and wonderfully well!" Still later the little me says, "But"— and you cut it off instantly. "No buts about it. I take my stand in the Omnipresent Christ I AM, and I permit no false beliefs or negative emotions to enter my consciousness. I refuse to play your silly game any longer!"

As Faith and Strength are developed, the Wisdom faculty will open beautifully, and you will be lifted up above the level of so-called common sense. Common sense is fine for the third-dimensional man or woman, but if you continue to work on that level, particularly out of a common sense of fear, you will never achieve mastery. For example, let's say that you must make a decision regarding your job or career, and common sense tells you to stay where you are because of the security. But what does Spirit have to say in the matter? You take the question within and ask for spiritual light and understanding, and your intuition may tell you to be bold and step out in faith—that the new career opportunity is truly the stepping stone to your True Place.

A friend of mine had a "gut feeling" to leave his secure and well-paying job as a CPA with a national firm and start a new and totally unrelated business. He followed the inner leading—taking a substantial reduction in income—but within a few years he was a multimillionaire. What he did was the perfect example of uncommon sense.

The Wisdom Center is an energy force located between the heart and solar plexus. As it becomes more vibrant, you will know what to do without going through a long and logical reasoning process. You will *feel* that a certain action is right—and you will move ahead without hesitation. The difference in good judgment and common sense? One is based on Spirit as *Cause*, while the other tends to draw support from the outer world of effects. If you are working with the Powers of Faith and Strength, you will not be fearful and overly cautious in taking actions—and at the same time you will not be compulsive or inconsiderate. Your actions will be guided by intuition and the inspiration of Spirit.

Remember that it is not your ego who is all-wise. As Socrates wrote: "The Delphic oracle said I was the wisest of all the Greeks. It is because I alone, of all the Greeks, know that I know nothing." And this is true of you, but when your Wisdom faculty is awakened, your consciousness becomes the channel through which the Wisdom, Understanding, and Knowledge of the Omniscient Christ Mind flows. And this is what it means to be an illumined One.

Spiritual Activity

Spiritual treatment for strength:

I am the Power of Strength. I am Power-full. I am strong in the mightiness of Spirit, and I am undaunted! My mind is firmly one-pointed in seeing only the good. My heart is fearless and knows only the emotion of victory. Nothing can touch me but the direct action of God, and God is my Omnipotent Self. I can do all things through the Strength of the Christ I AM. I AM Strength!

Spiritual treatment for wisdom:

I am the Power of Wisdom, and I call on this Power now to fill my heart and mind with the Light of perfect judgment and intuition. Through Christ in me, the very Spirit of God I AM, my actions are right and perfect. I know what to do at all times and in every situation. And I always do the right thing because it is the right thing to do! I know! I feel! And what I know and what I feel are Spiritual Knowledge and Inspiration guiding me every step of the way. God cannot make mistakes, and neither can I when I am consciously aware of the Presence within. I am now aware of that Presence, and I am filled and thrilled with the Illumination of Spirit. I AM Wisdom!

Chapter Sixteen

◆ ◈ ◆

The Power of Love

As we sit here in an imaginary circle, permit me to play back to certain ones of you what you have told me. Perhaps you did not speak these exact words, but to paraphrase Emerson, what you are in consciousness speaks louder than words. This is not judgment, for anything we can see in another we have seen in ourselves.

You think you can sit around with your nose out of joint and have others run around catering to you. You wear your feelings on your sleeves, and if everyone's actions do not fulfill your rigid expectations, you feel rejected. And you say that you are a practicing metaphysician!

And you with the short fuse. You call yourself a Truth student—which is synonymous with practicing the art of loving—but the only art you're developing is how to lose patience, get angry, and throw a good tantrum. And you wonder why your life is not whole and complete.

And you, the great hugger. You really know how to display affection in public, but the bitterness expressed behind your closed door is enough to keep your blood pressure high and maintain that pain in the neck in perfect order. Can you not love when you are alone?

And you, the "evolved" one. You say that you *know* Truth, and yet there is that deep resentment toward people of the past and present. Evolution comes through love, not the other way around.

And you with the sharp tongue. How you love to criticize your minister (not to his face, of course), but when asked what *your* ministry in life is, you say you can't get on with it because no one understands you. That's because you're not using the universal language of unconditional love.

And you, the fence straddler. The shift of your consciousness remains in neutral, and though you race the engine of your mind and emotions constantly, you go nowhere. And the reason is that you haven't begun to express your love nature, which is the go-power of the universe.

I could go on around the circle, but I think you get the point. If your life is not overflowing with abundance, wellness, and fulfillment, you are out of tune with the Love Vibration within you. If you *want* more out of life, you are going to have to *give* more to life. When you give more love, you receive the Kingdom.

Love is what created the universe, and Love is what the universe was created out of. Therefore, Love is Mind and also the thoughts of Mind. Love is the thrust of all creation. "And God said..." And the Word was Love, and the Power of the Word was Love, and the manifestation of the Power was Love. All *is* Love!

The Infinite All is the pure essence of Love. This Infinite Love thinks. Its Consciousness is perfect Love. As It contemplates Itself, It does so with Love. And what It sees, It loves. This

Father-Mother Mind conceived the perfect Image of Love, which became the first Principle, the ever-living male and female Principle, the I AM THAT I AM, the Love-Self-Reality of each one of us.

In the beginning, you knew only love. And your creations of materiality were born out of love, for you were a co-creator with God, bringing forth into manifestation only the Divine Ideas of Love. But once you began to identify yourself with your creations, you sealed off the Love Vibration with a material consciousness. Yet you continued to be, and will always be, a spiritual being of Love.

Some men and women have rediscovered (awakened to) their true nature of Love and have opened the inner door to receive once again the Energy of Love, letting it fill their consciousness and eliminate the error patterns of the past as light dissolves darkness. I call these people Superbeings.

Are you one? If you are, you know that you are Spirit, that Spirit is Love, and that Love is the activity of Spirit. You know that the activity of Spirit is Its Self-expression, and since your conscious awareness of Spirit is that Self-expression, you are pure Love. You know that the Love that created you forever sustains you.

Knowing that the Spirit of God—*your* Spirit—loves Its expression as your *Person*ality—you relax and let the burdens fall from your shoulders. Say to yourself:

Since the only Presence and Power of the Universe loves me and sustains me, what on earth could I possibly fear? Nothing. No-thing. Love heals. Love prospers. Love protects. Love guards. Love guides. Love restores. Love creates. Love makes all things new. So I let Love go before me now to straighten out every crooked place in

*my life. I place my faith in God's love for me, and I am
free, as I was created to be.*

Your God-Self will restore your life and transform your
world into a Garden of peace, joy, beauty, abundance, and fulfillment. But remember, you are a co-creator with God—not just an
empty projector through which images are thrown on the screen
of your world. You have a role to play, too, and that role is to be
a conscious participant as a radiating center of Divine Love.

Your "center"—which is another word for your energy
field—includes thoughts, feelings, words, and deeds. Therefore,
to be a co-creator with the Spirit of Love, you must think love,
feel love, speak love, and act with love. Your first thought of love
should be to respond to the love that your God-Self is eternally
pouring out upon you. Since this Presence within you loves you
with all of Its Divine Consciousness, should you not reciprocate
by loving this Reality of you with all your mind, your heart, your
strength? Can you not express gratitude for that love by returning
the love in full measure? When you do, the Connection is
restored, and the middle wall of partition is blown away.

Turn within and say:

*Thank you for loving me. Regardless of what I have
done in the past, I know that your love for me has never
diminished. Even when I ignored you, or blamed you, or
took action contrary to your counsel, you continued to
love me with all of your Being. I love your Love! And I
love You! My heart runneth over with love for You, my
Friend, my Guide, my Wonderful One, my Counselor, my
mighty God, my everlasting Father, my Prince of Peace,
my very Christ Self. Love is what I have received, and
Love is what I give, and I am now whole and complete.*

Since this God Presence within you *is* you—the Higher Self of you—and since this Self is forever expressing as the allness of you, can you now begin to love *all* of you from center to circumference? There is no place where God leaves off and you begin, so all is God, and all is you. *Know Thyself!* To know yourself is to love yourself—all the way through. And do not think that you are not worthy, because your worthiness is God's Worthiness. *Love Thyself!*

Think beautiful thoughts about yourself:

I am a delightful Child of God. My Spirit is God being me in the absolute. My conscious awareness of the indwelling Presence—my illumined personality—is God being me in expression. My body is God being me in physical form. I am God being me!

Knowing that everything I have ever done, ever said, ever thought, ever felt was simply my consciousness in action, I understand that I could not have expressed any differently. I was acting out of my consciousness; therefore, I dismiss all thoughts of right and wrong. That was simply where I was at the time, and I know now that my consciousness is evolving and I am returning Home to the Light of Love.

So I no longer condemn me. I no longer hold any unforgiveness toward myself. I rise above all feelings of guilt, and I am free to love myself as never before. I love this person I am with all my mind. I love this Individual I am with all my heart. My love for me, myself, the I that I AM, knows no bounds. I am Love. I am Love. I am Love.

You are told to love your neighbor as yourself, and your "neighbor" means every other soul on this planet and beyond, and all forms of life throughout the universe. So now turn your attention to the world and begin to radiate the Love Rays. When you direct the beams from the Love Energy Center of your heart, they go before you to transform every negative situation your neighbor may be experiencing into a splendid positive. This is Power-Love, rather than cuddly, fuzzy love, and there is nothing it cannot do. When you direct it toward anyone or anything, it literally changes the energy field in and around the person, place, or thing. This is God in action, peeling away the illusion and revealing the Reality.

Say to yourself:

> I will do my part to love my neighbor without exception. As I scan my consciousness, my mind picks up certain individuals of the past and present who evoke less-than-desirable emotions in me. I now transmute that negative energy by forgiving them and speaking words of unconditional love. (Speak the name aloud)...I love you! I love you unconditionally! I love you for Who and What you are with no strings attached. I am love. You are love. We are one in love, and we are healed through love. I now bring into my consciousness my home and family, my place of work, my city, state, and country, my world— and I send forth the Love Rays to heal and harmonize every negative condition on this planet. I feel the love pouring forth from my heart center, and I know that this Love Power will accomplish that for which it is sent. I am Love in Action!

Spiritual Activity

Spend time daily with the affirmative prayers in this chapter, then continue to be Love in action. *Be* God in action! Do not get caught in the mesmerism of listening and watching others fight, fume, and spew negative energy. Begin to pour love into the situation from your heart chakra, radiating it with intensity, and joyfully watch as the individuals are touched by the harmonizing rays. If injustice comes within the range of your consciousness, send forth the spiritual Energy of Love and see right action taking place. Use the Love Power in your home, your office, in the grocery store, the restaurants, the hospitals, the courtrooms, on the freeways—and notice how the environment changes. Stop being a spectator. Use your Love Rays in the service of Godkind to reveal order, harmony, and peace in this world.

Practice the use of Love-Power daily, and prove to yourself that you do indeed have a divine "zapper" at your disposal. If an insect bites you, focus the love energy at the point of contact and feel the instant relief from the sting. If you meet someone in a bad mood, throw open your heart and begin to pour out unconditional love with great purpose of mind and watch as darkness changes to light. You can *love* a failing business back to life. You can *love* a diseased body back to wellness. And you can *love* a negative condition right out of existence.

The act (feeling) of unconditional love opens the heart chakra and propels the harmonizing energy directly into the low vibratory force field and begins to "perk up" the vibration, literally lifting it to the Divine Standard. If you will just practice the procedure, you will be amazed at the results. Don't just think about it—do it!

When you are not purposely using your Love-Power, continue to *be* the Presence of Love. For example, can the Presence of

Love experience hurt feelings? Can Individualized Love feel rejected? Does a Master of Love attack out of anger? Would a Being of Love feel bitterness or resentment? Would God's perfect expression of Love condemn or criticize? You know the answers. Begin to live as the Love you are in Truth.

You might also spend some time in meditation reflecting on what Paul said about love in his letter to the Christians at Corinth:

> *If I speak with the eloquence of men and of angels, but have no love, I become no more than blaring brass or crashing cymbals. If I have the gift of foretelling the future and hold in my mind not only all human knowledge but the very secrets of God, and if I also have that absolute faith which can move mountains, but I have no love, I amount to nothing at all. If I dispose of all that I possess, yes, even if I give my own body to be burned, but have no love, I achieve nothing.*
>
> *This love of which I speak is slow to lose patience— it looks for a way of being constructive. It is not possessive: It is neither anxious to impress nor does it cherish inflated ideas of its own importance.*
>
> *Love has good manners and does not pursue selfish advantage. It is not touchy. It does not keep account of evil or gloat over the wickedness of other people. On the contrary, it is glad with all good men when truth prevails.*
>
> *Love knows no limit to its endurance, no end to its trust, no fading of its hope; it can outlast anything. It is, in fact, the one thing that still stands when all else has fallen.*

Chapter Seventeen

◆ ◆ ◆

Your Role
as the Christ

We must remember—through the awakening process—how to be the Masters we were created to be. We must understand the principle of supply so that we are not affected by anything that happens to the economic system. We must demonstrate radiant health so that we will have the energy and vitality to fulfill our purpose here. We must live under Divine Protection so that we may be in a safety zone at all times. We must reopen the Wisdom faculty within so that we may be guided to take the right action at the right time and in the right way. And we must be a beacon of illumination for others seeking the spiritual path.

Too difficult a task for you? No, it really isn't. You can truly step out in mastery this very day *if you choose to do so.* I am not talking about strutting around like a peacock and calling yourself a Lord. I am referring to your acceptance of your true Identity this day, and letting that Identity live through you every single moment of your eternal life.

You see, Christhood is not something to come at a point in the future when you are more evolved. Christhood *is*—right now. I am the Christ of God. You are the Christ of God. We were *Christed* in the beginning, and nothing and no one can ever take that away from us. And while it is true that a part of us is asleep and under the spell of illusion, there is so much more of us that is fully awake, fully illumined, and living the Reality of Truth— right now.

You are not having problems, and you are not facing challenges. You never have and you never will. You are whole and complete. Abundance is yours, wellness is yours, loving and harmonious relationships are yours, total fulfillment is yours, and you are enjoying the exquisite perfection of God's Universe at this very moment. In Truth, you never left the Father's house, you never fell from grace, and you certainly were not tossed out of some garden and told to till the ground until you dropped dead.

Before you say that I have you mixed up with someone else, let me remind you that you are the offspring of the Infinite Mind and Power of the Universe, and all that this Infinite Mind and Power is, you are. For God's sake, *know this.* You finally got through the worm-of-the-dust fixation, but you are still hanging in there with the obscene notion that you are a pawn of fate fighting for your good in a hostile world.

The reason you are still playing the illusion game is that you are living out of the lower ego consciousness, but you don't have to. At any time in the last two thousand years you could have risen into the vibration of the Soul and regained your realization of oneness with God. In fact, you have touched this Christ Vibration in moments of meditation, but you did not lock into it.

You took the elevator up, but instead of stepping out in mastery, you pushed the down button.

Regaining spiritual consciousness is not tearing one house down and building another. It is more like moving out of the basement and into the main floor. Remember that you are an individualized Energy Field. Within this force field are lower and higher vibrations. Your "I" of identity is like the mercury in a thermometer, rising and falling according to the weather of your thoughts and emotions. For the majority of people, the "I" remains in the cold, dark atmosphere of the ego, while all the time in the upper region of the energy field the Sun is shining and there is the warmth of Light, Love, and Joy. Here, the energy is pure, the vibrations high, and the Consciousness illumined.

But understand that this illumined Consciousness that is alive and living simultaneously with your mortal mind is *your* Consciousness. You cannot break a beam of light into parts. It's all one stream of radiance. When you lift up the "I" and move into this spiritual dimension of your own energy field, you do not lose consciousness and wake up as a stranger in a strange land. You do not trade one mind in for another. No, you take your consciousness with you and rise up into a new range of awareness, understanding, and knowledge.

As your thinking and feeling natures move up to a different coordinate in your energy field, you take on the Consciousness of the Higher Self, and the dark energies of the ego are transmuted. And while there were two states of consciousness before (duality), there is now only one. It is this energy of the Holy Self that says, "No one cometh unto the Father but by me." When you are in this spiritual vibration, you are literally in tune with the Infinite because God dwells in that vibration. And on this higher frequency you are fully aware of the Living Christ of your Being.

As you rise into this finer vibration, you become aware of your God-Self as never before. You sense that intense Knowingness. You see the brilliance of the indwelling Light. You feel the fire of that boundless love within you. And as your ego is swallowed up in this dimension of pure spiritual energy, you come into the fullness of the Christ Consciousness that says, "I am the Light of the world. I am the resurrection and the life." Now you *know* the Reality of your Self. Now you know that *you* are the Omnipotent Christ.

Spiritual Activity

Will you begin the ascension today? Will you accept the Truth of your Divine Identity and begin to act the role of the Christ? Will you play the part? If you will, even though you may at this moment be wallowing with the swine, I assure you that the robe and ring will be yours sooner than you can possibly imagine. How do you play the role? With everything you've got!

You take the thought into your mind that you are the Christ of God and you *live* with that thought throughout the day. And from that parent thought will come mental children of great love, joy, faith, understanding, power, strength, wisdom, forgiveness, imagination, will, life, and enthusiasm. And if you momentarily "forget your lines"—ask yourself—how does the Christ think? And let the thoughts flow.

How does the Christ feel? With total and complete unconditional love—so begin this day to love everyone and everything as you have never loved before. *Feel* that love vibration. Let it flow, pour out, radiate from you. *Be* the Love of God in action. And if your emotions pause for a moment to be anxious and fearful, just remind yourself that those are not Christ-like feelings, and as the

Christ of God, you will feel only joyous, peaceful, loving, and happy emotions.

How does the Christ speak? With words that represent the attributes of God. So your words will be kind, loving, compassionate, fearless, wise, joyous. Not one word will come forth from your mouth that denies the Divinity of yourself or your fellow beings. Criticism is not a part of your nature; there is never a verbal attack. Right thinking precedes your words and your conversations are always uplifting and inspiring. Your voice is as music to ears eager for the message of Truth.

How does the Christ act? With actions that reflect illumination, love, power, and perfect faith. Whenever there is an appearance of lack or limitation, you will give thanks for the infinite givingness of Spirit, and you will decree the Truth by recognizing the Reality behind the illusion. You will command the very energy of your being, the substance of your Self, to appear as the needed form or experience. Whenever you see conflict and hostility, you will radiate the Light of Love as a laser beam to harmonize the situation. Whenever there is the appearance of disease, you will send forth the Light of Truth with intense radiation to dissolve the error pattern and release the Healing Force from within the individual.

Remember, you are the Christ of God. Therefore, you will walk as the Christ, sit as the Christ, stand as the Christ. Your body language will reflect the Christ. Your facial expressions will reflect the Christ. And you will see everyone else as you see yourself—as the Christ of God, God in individual expression.

Can you play the role? If you can, something very mystical and beautiful will happen to you. The "I" of identity will begin to rise, moving from the dark, cold atmosphere of ego right up into the Kingdom of the Fourth Dimension. Even now you hear the call: "I am the bread of life. He that comes to me shall never hunger, and he that believes on me shall never thirst. You are from beneath; I am from above. Come unto me now."

I now return to the glory that I knew in the beginning. It is done.

PART III

YOUR ROLE AS A PLANETARY HEALER

"There is one thing stronger than all the armies of the world and that is an idea whose time has come."
— Voltaire

Chapter Eighteen

The Future Is Now

The book you are reading was originally titled *The Planetary Commission*—published by The Quartus Foundation in 1984—and "The Future Is Now" was Chapter One of that book. The objective was to lay the foundation for announcing World Healing Day on December 31, 1986. Since then, participating members of the Commission have grown into hundreds of millions, but we have only scratched the surface. For those of you who are not familiar with the mission and purpose of this annual global mind-link, here is an edited version of that original call for planetary healers. Hopefully you—with your uplifted consciousness of mastery—will join us by accepting your appointment to the Planetary Commission. There is so much more to do.

◆ ◆ ◆

We are living on a planet, a spaceship called Earth, suspended in a vast and infinite entity called space. And even though millions of people are on the Path of Love and Light and Peace and are dedicating their lives to Truth, there are still billions of men, women, and children caught in a competitive struggle just to survive. And in this struggle, each individual thinks, feels, and acts; and this mental-emotional-physical activity is registered in each individual energy field, in each consciousness. And because we are all one in every sense of the word, every single impulse in consciousness is impressed and registered in the collective consciousness of humankind—the universal energy field referred to as the race mind.

Now we know the power of one individual consciousness. We know that each one of us can affect matter and change space-time itself. We do that each day—from a positive standpoint—in our meditations, prayers, and spiritual treatments. We have seen evidence of incredible changes in the body as the appearance of disease is eliminated and physical organism is restored to health—sometimes instantly. We have also seen miraculous demonstrations of prosperity, true place success, and healed relationships where time and space were condensed to manifest a present reality. But we also know what our negative thinking and false beliefs can do—how fear, self-condemnation, unforgiveness, criticism, and resentment toward others can alter our physical structure and manifest as lack and limitation in our lives. Through the law of attraction, we can bring to us that which we fear the most, and hostility toward our brothers will set up such a negative vibration in our individual energy field that accidents, failure, broken relationships, and other shattering experiences will be drawn into our lives.

Now just imagine what billions of us could do grouped together in an energy field of negative consciousness. We could cover the world in a blanket of cold never before experienced in our history. We could send storms rolling over the country to erode beaches, flood farmland and cities, destroy homes and businesses, kill people, and cause damages in the billions of dollars. And we could stimulate suicide bombers, establish a reign of terrorism, and cause such intense distrust between nations with the greatest weapon technology that most of the world would live in a state of panic. This is exactly what we have done, and when I say "we," I am speaking of each one of us as representatives of humanity—as cells within the collective consciousness of humankind.

To answer the question—"Where do we go from here?"—we have to know where we want to go and what we want to be. So let's create the picture of our destination in our minds. Just imagine a world where there is no conflict—no selfish competition—only loving cooperation. Imagine a world free of pollution, free of want, free of disease, free of disaster. Imagine a world populated with smiling, laughing, happy, joyous people—all radiantly healthy, all abundantly supplied, all loved and loving. Get the feel of such a world, and put yourself right in the middle of it. Think of yourself as filled with life and energy and vitality, with a body that is strong and vibrant. See yourself surrounded with abundance and enjoying true prosperity. See yourself doing what you love and loving what you do, unbound and free. See yourself with the capacity to embrace and love and serve every single man and woman and child on this planet, regardless of who they are or what they have done—and feel that unconditional love radiating from you to all, and returning from all to you. And then see everyone in the world as you have seen yourself in the ideal.

From this image of peace and plenty in our minds, the next step is to make it a present reality with action. During 1983, my wife, Jan, and I meditated on the idea of "what can we do" for several months, and were led to establish a Planetary Commission to heal and harmonize the collective consciousness of humankind. The word *commission* in this case simply means a group of people appointed to perform a specific duty. Each individual desiring to be a part of the commission must make a definite commitment to do so, and the "appointment" is automatic with the commitment. All that we asked was for people to make a definite and dedicated commitment in writing to be a part of the healing, harmonizing influence for the salvation of this planet.

The Commission is not like any other kind of movement. We are not protesting or resisting anything. We are simply consenting to letting God be God—and we are volunteering to co-create with God in the implementation of the Divine Plan for each one of us and for all humanity.

To serve as a Light Bearer on the Commission requires no dues. There is no organizational structure. There will be no meetings. However, at Noon Greenwich time on December 31st of each year—continuing until the race mind shifts—men, women, and children all over the world will gather in a global mind-link to release love, light, and spiritual energy into that collective consciousness.

The first formal announcement of the Commission was made on January 1, 1984, with the idea of building momentum for an hour of spiritual oneness on the last day of 1986. Why Noon Greenwich and December 31st? We chose the time because that hour would encompass all time zones around the world during the 24-hour period, giving the simultaneous mind-link full impact. The date was given during meditation as the day representing a certain alignment of energies providing a "window" into the race consciousness. And 1986 was designated as the year because we had been told in meditation that 1987 would be the year of the *critical mass*.

You see, throughout our history, the mass of dark energy in the race mind has been subcritical in that the chain reaction of negative consequences has not been self-sustaining. But the density of the force field was increasing—to reach a point where the darkness exceeded the light, the positive balance lost, and the negative chain reaction going critical—and this self-sustaining action was predicted for 1987.

Our objective was obvious. Why not reverse the polarity of the force field and achieve a critical mass of positive energy? Why not insure a chain reaction of self-sustaining Good in and around and through this planet? In order to reach the critical mass of spiritual consciousness, our objective by December 1986 was to have 500 million people on earth simply consenting to a healing of this planet and to the reign of spiritual Love and Light in this world—with no less than 50 million meditating at the same time on December 31, 1986. It was our feeling that the larger group, which would serve as the main body of the Commission and represent about 10 percent of the global population, would not only maintain the negative energy mass in a sub-critical state, but would also begin to break up the severe intensity of the "dark pockets"—thus preparing the collective consciousness for the massive penetration of Light on the final day of 1986.

The Seeds of Peace Were Sown on December 31, 1986

Perhaps the best summary of the 1986 Event was found in the *Los Angeles Times*:

> It was billed as the biggest participatory event in history. The grass roots World Peace Event on Wednesday called upon peace activists to band together for a common cause: to spend an hour praying for world peace.

And that's what millions of them did between 4 and 5 A.M. PST, an hour when it was New Year's Eve in all the world's time zones.

They gathered in ashrams and town squares in India, at mountaintop ski resorts in Colorado, in churches and temples in San Diego and in the privacy of their own homes...to ring in what they hope will be the beginning of a new era of world harmony.

In New York City, public radio station WBAI carried a satellite hookup with the Soviet Union to celebrate the World Peace Event. The four-hour special featured entertainment provided by artists from the East and West, and included greetings of peace and the reading of a Soviet child's letter to President Reagan about the need to eliminate nuclear arms.

Event organizers based the estimate of the large response—150 million to 400 million—on a computer analysis of information from sources worldwide.

(Excerpted from articles written by *Los Angeles Times* staff writers Maria L. La Ganga and Dennis McLellan.)

Based on signed commitments, people representing all major religious faiths from 77 countries on 7 continents in 524 organizations were a part of this hour of global cooperation. Peace ceremonies were held in cities throughout North and South America, Europe, Asia, Africa, India, and Australia—in arenas, stadiums, city parks, churches, temples, ashrams, hotel ballrooms, capitol rotundas, forests, on mountains and beaches, and in private homes. Many governors and mayors in the U.S. issued proclamations designating December 31st as World Peace Day.

The Commission did not disband after December 31, 1986. Between 500 million and 800 million of the world's citizens came together on the annual World Healing Days of 1987 and 1988, and the activity has expanded and gathered strength each year since—encouraged greatly by a report from the Stockholm International Peace Research Institute. Walter Stuetzle, the Institute's director and a former West German Undersecretary of Defense, said that "1988 has seen remarkable progress toward a potentially more peaceful world...there was a clear break in the pattern of a constant increase in the number of major conflicts with which the world had grown accustomed during the 1980s."

It was Mikhail Gorbachev who said, "We need a revolution of the mind." And in later naming Gorbachev Man of the Decade, *Time* magazine reported that "the metaphysics of global power has changed." It certainly had, with Hungry, East Germany, Poland, Czechoslovakia, Rumania, and Bulgaria coming out of the cold and joining a new global society. And when the symbol of the Iron Curtain—the Berlin Wall—was turned into souvenirs, we were shown not only the "revolution of the mind" manifesting as a physical reality, but also the power of the mind-link to dissolve old forms and structures.

We also saw the release of Nelson Mandela and the destruction of the pillars of apartheid in South Africa, and the 300,000 students and citizens demanding more democracy in China. True, the democracy movement in China was quashed and thousands of protesters were killed or wounded, but the seeds of freedom were planted for a magnificent future harvest. There was also the peace agreement signed by the presidents of Central America, the first presidential election held in Chile since 1970, and the elections in Nicaragua and the defeat of the Sandinistas.

Many more positive events could be added to the list, but as we read the newspapers now in the late 1990s, we see that our work has just begun—and that's why the Commission is an ongoing global activity. With continued dedication to peace, this world can be totally transformed, and we ask you to participate in three ways:

1. Make a dedicated effort to practice and express peace on a daily basis, realizing that peace must begin within the heart and mind of each individual.

2. Reserve one hour on the last day of each month to meditate on peace. This need not take place at noon Greenwich time; any one-hour period that is most convenient for you will be satisfactory.

3. Meet again in spirit for the Annual Global Mind-Link at noon Greenwich time, December 31st—and continue it at the same time on the last day of every year until the last one comes into the Light.

Regarding the third point, take action to spread the word about the event. Plan in advance, and fully publicize any public gatherings, and enlist the support of community and religious leaders in your area. Discuss the plans at school functions and in civic and social organizations. Do whatever is necessary to create a positive awareness of World Healing Day and an understanding that each individual can make a world of difference.

The form identifying you as a member of the Commission is included in the Appendix. Please sign it as your commitment to world healing, and use it as a reminder of your mission. Then begin to radiate the Christ Spirit you are in Truth to this world. Open your heart and let Divine Love pour out to one and all, transmuting every negative situation within the range of your consciousness. Forgive everyone, including yourself. Forgive the past and close the door.

Let there be peace in your heart, the excitement of victory in your mind, and joyous words on your lips. Turn within and see and find and know the only Presence, the only Power, the only Cause, and the only Activity of your eternal life. Be a totally open channel for the glorious expression of this infinite You!

And then on December 31st, join with billions around the world in the healing meditation. Don't just be a spectator. The addition of your individual light may be just the one to alter the balance and achieve the critical mass of spirituality.

The salvation of the world *does* depend on you!

APPENDIX

- ◆ Your Appointment to the Planetary Commission

- ◆ The Time Where You Are at Noon Greenwich Time

- ◆ The World Healing Meditation

- ◆ Questions and Answers

I ACCEPT MY APPOINTMENT
TO THE PLANETARY COMMISSION

I choose to be a part of the Planetary Commission, and I do hereby consent to the healing and harmonizing of this planet and all forms of life hereon.

I shall begin this day to radiate the Infinite Spirit I AM in Truth to this world. I open my heart and I let Divine Love pour out to one and all, transmuting every negative situation and experience within the range of my consciousness.

I forgive everyone, including myself. I forgive the past, and I close the door. From this moment on, I shall dedicate my life to turning within and seeking, finding, and knowing the only Presence, the only Power, the only Cause, and the only Activity of my eternal life. And I place my faith in the Presence of God within as my Spirit, my Substance, my Supply, and my Support.

I know that as I lift up my consciousness, I will be doing my part to cancel out the error of the race mind, heal the sense of separation, and restore the world to sanity.

With love in my heart, the thrill of victory in my mind, and joyous words on my lips, I agree to be a part of the worldwide group that will meet in spirit at noon Greenwich time on December 31st of each year to release Light, Love, and Spiritual Energy in the Healing Meditation for Planet Earth.

_____   _____
Date   **Signature**

TIME ZONES

◆ ◈ ◆

United States Times Zones

Noon Greenwich Time

Pacific Standard Time	4:00 A.M.
Mountain Standard Time	5:00 A.M.
Central Standard Time	6:00 A.M.
Eastern Standard Time	7:00 A.M.

Noon Greenwich Time in Various Cities of the World

Berlin	1:00 P.M.	Montreal	7:00 A.M.
Buenos Aires	9:00 A.M.	Moscow	3:00 P.M.
Cairo	2:00 P.M.	Naples	1:00 P.M.
Copenhagen	1:00 P.M.	Nome	1:00 A.M.
Edmonton	5:00 A.M.	Ottawa	7:00 A.M.
Fairbanks	2:00 A.M.	Paris	1:00 P.M.
Glasgow	Noon	Rome	1:00 P.M.
Honolulu	2:00 A.M.	Sydney	10:00 P.M.
London	Noon	Tokyo	9:00 P.M.
Madrid	1:00 P.M.	Vancouver	4:00 A.M.
Mexico City	6:00 A.M.	Vienna	1:00 P.M.

THE WORLD HEALING MEDITATION

In the beginning
In the beginning *God.*
In the beginning God created the heaven and the earth.
And God said Let there be light: and there was light.

Now is the time of the *new* beginning.
I am a co-creator with God, and it is a new Heaven that
        comes, as the Good Will of God is expressed on
        Earth through me.
It is the Kingdom of Light, Love, Peace, and Understanding.
And I am doing my part to reveal its Reality.

I begin with me.
I am a living Soul and the Spirit of God dwells in me, as me.
I and the Father are one, and all that the Father has is mine.
In Truth, I am the Christ of God.

What is true of me is true of everyone,
        for God is all and all is God.
I see only the Spirit of God in every Soul.
And to every man, woman, and child on Earth I say:
I love you, for you are me. You are my Holy Self.

I now open my heart, and let the pure essence of
        Unconditional Love pour out.

I see it as a Golden Light radiating from the center of my
being, and I feel its Divine Vibration in and through
me, above and below me.
I am one with the Light.
I am filled with the Light.
I am illumined by the Light.
I am the Light of the world.

With purpose of mind, I send forth the Light.
I let the radiance go before me to join the other Lights.
I know this is happening all over the world at this moment.
I see the merging Lights.
There is now one Light. We are the Light of the world.

The one Light of Love, Peace, and Understanding is moving.
It flows across the face of the Earth, touching and
illuminating every soul in the shadow of the illusion.
And where there was darkness, there is now the Light
of Reality.

And the Radiance grows, permeating, saturating every
form of life.
There is only the vibration of one Perfect Life now.
All the kingdoms of the Earth respond,
and the Planet is alive with Light and Love.
There is total Oneness,
and in this Oneness we speak the Word.
Let the sense of separation be dissolved.
Let mankind be returned to Godkind.

Let peace come forth in every mind.
Let love flow forth from every heart.
Let forgiveness rein in every soul.
Let understanding be the common bond.

And now from the Light of the world, the One Presence
and Power of the Universe responds.
The Activity of God is healing and harmonizing Planet
Earth.
Omnipotence is made manifest.

I am seeing the salvation of the Planet before my very eyes,
as all false beliefs and error patterns are dissolved.
The sense of separation is no more; the healing has taken
place, and the world is restored to sanity.

This is the beginning of Peace on Earth and Good Will
toward all, as Love flows forth from every heart,
forgiveness reigns in every soul, and all hearts and
minds are one in perfect understanding.

It is done. And so it is.

Questions and Answers

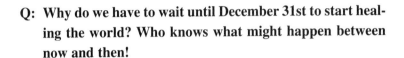

Q: Why do we have to wait until December 31st to start healing the world? Who knows what might happen between now and then!

A: Please refer again to the three-point Plan for Peace as discussed in Chapter Eighteen. Also, remember that you help the world when you lift up your consciousness and become one with the Christ Vibration within. So begin this day to clean up, clear out, and expand your consciousness, knowing that *you* can make a difference right now.

Q: What is the most effective form of meditation and spiritual treatment?

A: The one that works for you. Remember that your good already IS! You already have in the depths of your consciousness the spiritual prototype of everything you could possibly desire in the physical world. You role in the scheme of things is to clear your consciousness and become an open channel for the outpouring of your good. And the "way" to do this depends on your particular mind-set and vibration of consciousness. As you spend time with the spiritual activities in your workbook, and devote a period each day to contemplative meditation, you will open the door to the Secret Place. The Spirit within you guarantees it.

Q: Does the idea of "Superbeings" or "Masters" contribute to spiritual snobbery among New Age people?

A: If it does, it's that bloated ego getting in the way again. Please understand this: Every individual on this planet, whether a New Thoughter, Mainliner, Fundamentalist, Catholic, Jew, Buddhist, Hindu, or whatever, is a master. No one is more spiritually advanced than another. The only difference is that some have awakened to their true Identity. The 12 phases of consciousness that I wrote about in *The Superbeings* are simply that—phases in the awakening process. Some of our brothers and sisters are asleep; they are sleeping masters. Some are awake; they are the awakened masters. And millions are just now coming out of the deep sleep. Let's call them drowsy masters.

As you work with this book to eliminate false beliefs, error patterns, and negative appearances, you will experience a rise in consciousness. And as you develop a greater awareness, understanding, and knowledge of the Christ within, your outer world will change accordingly. But even when total dominion comes, you will not be more advanced than your neighbor. In fact, the greater the spiritual evolvement, the greater the desire to serve. The higher you rise in consciousness, the more you will express unconditional love toward one and all. An Awakened One has no false pride or spiritual arrogance.

Q: Can we evolve in consciousness more rapidly through group activities?

A: If you mean *spiritual* groups, the answer is definitely yes.

The time of spiritual growth through total isolation is gone. It went out with the Age of Pisces. In the Aquarian Age, the Age of Spirituality, the emphasis is on two or more gathered together in the name and through the power of the indwelling Christ. This is why it is so important to get involved with a New Thought Church, study group, or a weekly class where experiences are shared. When the group is on the same vibration, spiritual treatments and "master minding" are very powerful, frequently overcoming the limitations of time and space in producing new conditions. And the sharing of energies can definitely enhance spiritual growth.

Q: Which spiritual teaching is right? I go to (name of church) and have read dozens of books, and I see contradictions in the teachings. I seem to be hopelessly confused.

A: They are *all* right in one aspect or another. Every metaphysical book, New Thought lecture, Ancient Wisdom teaching, or spiritual instruction is perfectly correct for *someone*. Every writer, teacher, minister, and counselor is coming from his or her belief system conditioned by personal growth and experience, religious training, inner guidance, and relationships with others. And regardless of how fundamental, conservative, advanced, progressive, or weird the instruction is, it is ideal for others who may be on that same frequency. No teaching is totally right or wrong, and on some level, every single contradiction comes into agreement.

I've looked at the writings of hundreds of different authors from the past and present and have found they were basically saying the same thing—all talking about the same mountain with just different ways to get to the top. We will all move past the confusion stage when we focus on the common denominator in all the teachings—that we are divine beings created by God and eternally one with our Source— and go from there, relying on our own inner guidance to show us the right path for where we are in consciousness at the time.

Q: Has your higher Self ever spoken to you in an audible voice?

A: A clear and strong audible voice filled my bedroom in the late 1970s with an instruction I will never forget. The words were: *Quiet trust!* I try to remember that when things seem to get a bit out of sync.

Q: Does anything ever bother you?

A: Certainly, and the "thing" is usually me. Remember it's not what happens that counts, but how you react to what happens. Sometimes I don't like my reactions.

Q: We hear so much today about "family values." What does that really mean from a metaphysical or spiritual perspective?

A: What does it mean from *any* perspective? Since the beginning of time, there's never been a family on earth that wasn't dysfunctional, which has led to a totally dysfunctional world. So how can we put a value on something that's abnormal, impaired, and incomplete? I'd rather place my values on the Reality of each person, whether family or not, and see the sacred, secret Essence of life, love, joy, peace, and wholeness in all. I might add that when we do this in the inner family circle, harmony becomes the natural state of the home.

Q: **Why is *soul* such a controversial word?**

A: Because of different perspectives and understanding. In traditional New Thought, soul (small *s*) is considered either the subconscious mind, or a combination of both conscious and subconscious. So the divine part of us, our Essential Self, is commonly referred to as Spirit rather than soul. In many of the ancient wisdom teachings, however, Soul (capital *S*) is synonymous with our Divine Consciousness, the I AM Self, our Spirit. It was also taught that we have an animal soul and a Divine Soul.

Personally, I like to work with the idea of Divine Self (Spirit) and Self-awareness (the illumined conscious mind). This is me being consciously aware of Me—consciousness recognizing Consciousness and becoming the channel through which the creative energy flows. The main thing is, don't get hung up on terms. Semantic traps can be like quicksand.

Q: **There are some current highly rated spiritual books that say reincarnation is not true, yet I've had a past-life regression and know it is. Please explain.**

A: In the Mind of God, reincarnation is not true. In the mind of humanity, it is. I addressed this in my book *With Wings As Eagles*[1], and offer this excerpt to help in your understanding:

Reincarnation was not a part of the Cosmic System—not a principle of the Plan of Creation. As man expressed in form and his consciousness of body expanded, the intensity of the awareness grew so strong that it became essentially hypnotic. So powerful was the focus that the form side of life became the principal means of self-identification. Knowledge and consciousness of Essence was replaced with a perception of man-as-form.

Except for a few Souls who retained the knowledge of consciously altering vibratory rates to lift the form into the higher energy—and there continues to be such people on the planet today—mankind was now imprisoned on the Earth plane. The cessation of vital functions of the physical vehicle was the only release, the only door to the higher realm. Even though the life-span was many times the average of today, the gradual lowering of the vibratory activity eventually affected disintegration of the form, and the Soul was liberated.

Once the earliest Souls were freed to return to the higher plane, there was an awareness that the original perfection of man could only be regained in the vibration where the ideal state was lost—the energy of Earth. Thus, the Spiritual Collective, man's own spiritual consciousness in oneness, established the Law of Rebirth. It is now a part of what you may call the Law of Evolution.

Most of the people in the world believe in reincarnation, and it is certainly a "fact of life."

Q: Is there a proper diet to help me grow spiritually?

A: The awakened ones have believed for aeons that your "diet" is energy—that food is for the etheric body and not the physical, for the etheric absorbs the energy of the food, while the function of the physical is to eliminate the food. (The etheric is that sheath of energy that surrounds the physical.) All eatables are essentially energy, yet the benefits or detriment of the energy elements within the form depend on where you are on the life cycle. Personally, I take no thought for what I eat and let the inner Intelligence select the nourishment. I believe that fanaticism in dieting or in the selection of foods is counter-productive to spiritual growth.

Q: At one of your workshops you spoke of a list of "precautions." Would you please repeat them for me?

A: They are:

Do not be overly exacting, overly careful, overly mental. Practice the sacred art of relaxation, of being care-less.

Do not engage in lamentation toward self, or accept the herd belief in physical deterioration.

Turn away from selfishness, greediness, ill-nature, malevolence, resentment, and hateful criticism. Be not caught in the whirlpool of alternating suppression and unrestrained desire fulfillment.

Strive for balance. Find the right proportions in life. See symmetry. Be at peace and develop order. When there is harmony, wholeness lives. Without harmony, the door to sickness is open.

Do not accept aging as a principle, or you will age.

Do not satisfy the desires of life through the substitution of food for the fulfillment of other yearnings, or the bones will suffer.

Do not refuse to see spirit within as the cause of all reality, or there will be friction in mind to affect the bloodstream.

Do not feel irritation towards a class or race of people or feel that you are abused, or you will be vulnerable to infections.

The points, or precautions, simply reflect the ancient teachings on how to stay well on the journey through life.

Q: Someone in our study group mentioned that the Scarlet Council had reappeared in America. What does that mean to you?

A: At one time in ancient Egypt, the priestcraft completely took over the country and corrupted the spiritual teachings of this great center of learning. They forced their own beliefs upon the people and required total obedience to their dogma, which became the national religion. They dominated national affairs, and the Pharaoh became a puppet in their hands. They quickly organized the systematic destruction of all ancient wisdom texts, and elaborate theologies were created to capture the minds of the people. This priesthood was known as the Scarlet Council. Perhaps the person was alluding to the mind-set of extreme fundamentalists in this country, whose agenda is to make America a Christian republic and not a democracy.

Q: **At an International New Thought Alliance (INTA) Conference. you gave your vision of the future. I can't find the tape and would appreciate hearing what you said.**

A: I hope reading it will help. As you read the words, let your mind penetrate the symbols, and expand your imagination to see and sense the fullness of the images while the feeling of love pours from your heart. Still yourself for a moment and imagine...

> *It is almost dawn and you are alone on a country road. There are hills on each side as far as the eye can see, and you notice the shapes of the trees standing tall in this first light. Smell the fresh, clean air as you begin to walk briskly down the road. Hear the songs of the birds, the music of daybreak. Feel the delight of a magnificent new day.*
>
> *You are so full of life and love that you exclaim, "Thank you, God, for the world that YOU have created, a world of peace, love, forgiveness, and understanding. Help us all to see this glorious reality, to KNOW it. Let every member of your family on this earth awaken to the glory that has been ours since the beginning of time. And let this world reflect only your vision, your truth. Let the dream be healed.*
>
> *And suddenly you catch sight of the brilliant sun rising in all its grandeur and majesty, and out of the corner of your eye you see someone walking down the hill to the road, followed by other men, women, and children. You look to the other side, and more and more people are streaming toward you. They*

join you, and you walk in step together, a spirited march of gladness and jubilation.

You look into the smiling faces and you realize that in the procession are Christians, Jews, Muslims, Hindus, Buddhists—people of all religions, nationalities, races, colors, and cultures. And as you look ahead, you see that the hills are now overspread with people, and you hear their songs of joy as they descend upon the road to merge with the assemblage.

You continue through the villages and towns, and without asking a question, the residents stop what they are doing and merge with the parade. You reach the busy highway connecting the cities, and the cars and trucks pull over and stop, the occupants joining in the march.

For just a moment, you think about the immensity of this gathering, and in your mind's eye you see that it is happening everywhere. In all the nations on earth, the people have united, all moving as one and following the sun, intuitively knowing that the old days, the old ways, will soon be gone forever.

As nightfall approaches in each country, the processions stop and the people rest. They know it is the last night of darkness, and all over the world people are gathering to spend this end time in grateful prayer and joyful meditation, waiting upon the birth of the New Day.

The final hour arrives, and the people of the planet stand together, awaiting the dawn. It comes. Slowly the light breaks through the darkness, the celestial voices heralding the Commencement, the music of the spheres proclaiming the New Beginning.

The people look into each other's eyes and lovingly embrace. The lambs and lions are now united, and harmony reigns. The healing light pervades, and sickness and sorrow are no more. The bountiful land feeds and nourishes all, and hunger is forgotten. There is now only perfect peace.

It is the time of the New World, the New Civilization. And the people are exceedingly glad.

Notes

CHAPTER ONE: Lessons to Learn, Lessons Learned

1. Alice A. Bailey, *Esoteric Astrology* (New York: Lucis Publishing Company, 1951), p. 18.

2. Dr. Douglas Baker, *The Jewel in the Lotus* (Herts, Eng.: Douglas Baker, 1974), p. 74.

CHAPTER TWO: Your Gifts and Talents

1. Dr. Douglas Baker, *The Jewel in the Lotus* (Herts, Eng.: Douglas Baker, 1974), p. 81.

2. Alice A. Bailer, *Esoteric Astrology* (New York: Lucis Publishing Company, 1951), p. 18.

3. John Randolph Price, *Angel Energy* (New York: Fawcett Columbine/Ballantine, 1995), p. 58.

4. Ibid.

CHAPTER THREE: Your Life Program

1. John Randolph Price, *The Superbeings* (trade edition: Carlsbad, CA.: Hay House, Inc., 1997; mass-market edition, New York: Fawcett Crest, Ballantine Books, 1988).

CHAPTER SIX: No Man's Land

1. John Randolph Price, *Empowerment* (Carlsbad, CA.: Hay House, Inc., 1996), p. 105.

CHAPTER SEVEN: The Choice Is Yours

1. John Randolph Price, *The Superbeings* (trade edition: Carlsbad, CA.: Hay House, Inc., 1997; mass-market edition, New York: Fawcett Crest, Ballantine Books, 1988), p. xxii.

CHAPTER TWELVE: Health and Healing

1. Louise L. Hay, *Heal Your Body* (Carlsbad, CA.: Hay House, Inc., 1988), p. 3.

QUESTIONS AND ANSWERS

1. John Randolph Price, *With Wings As Eagles* (Carlsbad, CA.: Hay House, Inc., 1997), pp. 23-24.

About the Author

◆ ◆ ◆

John Randolph Price is the co-founder with his wife, Jan, of The Quartus Foundation, a spiritual research and communications organization formed in 1981. Prior to the founding of Quartus, John devoted more than 25 years to the advertising and public relations business, serving as executive vice president of a Chicago agency, and president of a Houston-based firm.

He began researching the philosophic mysteries of Ancient Wisdom in the mid-1960s, and he has integrated those teachings with spiritual psychology and metaphysics in the writing of his many books. In 1994, he was presented the International New Thought Alliance's Joseph Murphy Award in recognition of the contribution that his books have made to positive living throughout the world.

For information about workshops conducted by John and Jan Price, and their monthly publications, please contact **The Quartus Foundation, P.O. Box 1768, Boerne, TX 78006.**

We hope you enjoyed this Hay House book.
If you would like to receive a free catalog featuring
additional Hay House books and products,
or if you would like information about the
Hay Foundation, please contact:

Hay House, Inc.
P.O. Box 5100
Carlsbad, CA 92018-5100

(800) 654-5126
(800) 650-5115 (fax)

Please visit the Hay House Website at:
http://www.hayhouse.com